Dishcloths *to Crochet*

Fun Designs to Brighten Your Kitchen!

Pat Olski

Dover Publications, Inc.
Mineola, New York

Dedicated to the memory
of my admirable and beloved cousin
Kamil Patel

INTRODUCTION

Crocheting dishcloths is a relaxing, enjoyable activity, and one that can be a welcome diversion from crocheting a more serious project. What can be more satisfying than crocheting a project that requires a minimal amount of thread, can be completed in a day or two, and results in an appealing and useful item? Attractive and useful in your own kitchen, they are wonderful little gifts for a shower or a housewarming, as well as inexpensive yet personal birthday or holiday presents. In this collection of twenty-five delightful patterns, you'll be sure to find a dishcloth to suit every personality or occasion.

Some of the designs in this book are so simple that they can be used to teach a beginner of any age to crochet. In fact, the distinctive and whimsical motifs are perfectly suited to fire a child's imagination, and the projects can be completed quickly to maintain a child's interest. Since each project is so small and self-contained, the successful outcome of the project does not depend upon the gauge. Each dishcloth will vary in size depending upon the type of thread you choose and the tightness (or looseness) of your stitches. A novice in the art of the crochet hook can begin their first lesson fashioning Sweet Strawberry for instance; a more experienced crocheter will find the more elaborate dishcloths, such as Handsome Horse, a bit more challenging. But whatever your level of expertise, you'll find many projects in this book gratifying, both while crocheting them and while enjoying them after completion.

Patterns revised by Pat Olski

Photographs by Brian Kraus

Bibliographical Note

Dishcloths to Crochet: Fun Designs to Brighten Your Kitchen!, first published by Dover Publications, Inc., in 2018, is a selection of patterns chosen from *Crocheting Novelty Pot Holders*, which was originally published by Dover in 1982. The 25 patterns have all been updated and revised for this edition.

Library of Congress Cataloging-in-Publication Data

Names: Olski, Pat, author.
Title: Dishcloths to crochet : fun designs to brighten your kitchen! / Pat Olski.
Description: Mineola, New York : Dover Publications, Inc., [2018] | "Is a
   selection of patterns chosen from Crocheting Novelty Pot Holders (1982).
   The 25 patterns have all been updated and revised for this edition."
Identifiers: LCCN 2017055230| ISBN 9780486817293 | ISBN 0486817296
Subjects: LCSH: Crocheting—Patterns. | Potholders.
Classification: LCC TT820 .O39 2018 | DDC 746.43/4041—dc23
LC record available at https://lccn.loc.gov/2017055230

Manufactured in the United States by LSC Communications
81729601   2018
www.doverpublications.com

CONTENTS

ABBREVIATIONS

ch	chain stitch
dc	double crochet
dc2tog	double crochet 2 stitches together
dc3tog	double crochet 3 stitches together
dtr	double treble st
hdc	half double crochet
lp(s)	loop(s)
MC	main color
mm	millimeter(s)
oz	ounce(s)
PC	popcorn st
prev	previous
PS	puff stitch
rnd(s)	round(s)
RS	right side
sc	single crochet
sc2tog	single crochet 2 stitches together
sc3tog	single crochet 3 stitches together
sk	skip
sl st	slip stitch
sp(s)	space(s)
st(s)	stitch(es)
tr	treble crochet st
pm	place marker
wyoh	wrap yarn over hook
WS	wrong side
yd	yard(s)
yoh	yarn over hook

BASIC DIRECTIONS TO MAKE A HANGING LOOP

Using DK/worsted yarn and 4.00/5.00mm hook:
Wrap yarn around two fingers five times to form a loop.
Remove the loop from fingers, and pinch it to keep the strands together.
Sc over loop, packing stitches tightly together until loop is covered. Sl st into first sc to join. Fasten off, leaving yarn tail to sew to dishcloth.

Using Size 5 cotton and 2.00mm hook:
Wrap thread around two fingers eight times to form a loop.
Remove the loop from fingers, and pinch it to keep the strands together.
Sc over loop, packing stitches tightly together until loop is covered. Sl st into first sc to join. Fasten off, leaving yarn tail to sew to dishcloth.

Using Size 10 cotton and 1.75/1.80mm hook:
Wrap thread around two fingers ten times to form a loop.
Remove the loop from fingers, and pinch it to keep the strands together.
Sc over loop, packing stitches tightly together until loop is covered. Sl st into first sc to join. Fasten off, leaving yarn tail to sew to dishcloth.

Cheeky *Chicken*

CHICKEN

Body

Using MC start at top. Ch 68.

Row 1: Sc 1 in second ch from hook, *sk 2 ch, dc 5 in next ch (shell made), sk 2 ch, sc in next ch; rep from * across. Turn—11 shells.

Rows 2 & 6: Ch 3, *sc in center (3rd) dc of next shell, shell in back loop of next sc; rep from * across, ending with 3 dc (half shell) in last sc. Turn.

Rows 3, 4, 7 & 8: Ch 1, sc in first dc, *shell in back loop of next sc, sc in center dc of next shell; rep from * across, ending with a half shell in back loop of last sc. Turn.

Rows 5 & 9: Ch 1, sc 1 in first dc, *shell in back loop of next sc, sc in center dc of next shell; rep from * across, ending with 2 dc in back loop of last sc. Turn.

Row 10: Ch 1, *sc 1 in center dc of next shell, shell in back loop of next sc; rep from * across, ending with 2 dc in back loop of last sc. Turn.

Row 11: Ch 1, sc 1 in first dc, *shell in back loop of next sc, sc in center dc of next shell; rep from * across. Turn.

Row 12: Ch 3, *sc 1 in center dc of next shell, shell in back loop of next sc; rep from * across, ending with 2 dc in back loop of last sc. Turn.

Row 13: Ch 3, dc 1 in first sc, *sc in center dc of next shell, shell in back loop of next sc; rep from * across, ending with a sc in last shell. Turn.

Row 14: Ch 3, *sc in center dc of next shell, shell in back loop of next sc; rep from * across, ending with a sc in top of ch-3 of prev row. Turn.

Rows 15–17: Ch 3, *sc in center of next shell, shell in back loop of next sc; rep from * across, ending with sc in center dc of last shell. Turn.

Fasten off.

Attach MC to first sc on first row and, working over slanted end, sc 44 sts across to opposite end. Fasten off. Attach color A to sc, hdc 9, dc 24, hdc 5, sc 5.

Fasten off.

Head

Using MC, ch 5, sl st to form ring.

FINISHED SIZE

3½in/9cm high (center of body) x 8in/20cm wide (from side of head to tip of tail)

YARN

DMC® *Cébélia Crochet Cotton Thread Size 10*: 1.75oz/50g, 284yds/260m (100% mercerized cotton)—one ball each: #800 Pale Delft (MC), #799 Medium Delft (A), #603 Bright Pink (B)

Small amounts of black yarn and yellow yarn for embroidery

NOTIONS

- Size 6 (1.80mm) crochet hook *or size needed to obtain gauge*
- Tapestry needle

GAUGE

24 sts and 28 rows = 4in/10cm over sc
Take time to check gauge.

STITCH GLOSSARY

Shell: Dc 5 in the back loop of the next st.

Half Shell: Dc 3 in the back loop of the next st.

Note: Instructions are for one wing and one eye. If two eyes and wings are made, the dishcloth can be reversible.

Rnd 1: Ch 3, dc 14 in ring, sl st into ch-3 to join.

Rnd 2: Ch 3, dc into ch-3 from prev rnd, dc 2 in each dc around, sl st to join rnd into ch-3.

Rnd 3: Ch 3, dc into ch-3 from prev rnd (counts as 2 dc), *dc in next dc, dc 2 in next dc; rep from * around, sl st to join rnd into ch-3—45 sts.

Rnd 4: Ch 1, sc into ch-3 from prev rnd, sc 34, hdc in same place as last sc, hdc in next dc, dc 9, sl st into first sc. Turn.

Shape Neck

Row 1: Ch 4, tr 2, dc 1, hdc 1, sc 7. Turn.

Row 2: Ch 3, skip first, sc, dc 5, tr 5. Turn.

Row 3: Ch 4, [tr 1, dc 1] in next st, dc 2, hdc 4, sc across to end.

Fasten off. Long edge is back of neck.

Comb

Using color B, attach yarn to the 4th stitch on head from back of neck.

Row 1: Ch 1, sc 2 in next sc, sc 1, hdc 1, [dc 1, 2 dc in next sc] 6 times. Turn.

Row 2: Ch 2, sc 2 in second ch from hook, skip first dc, sc in next dc, *ch 2, sc in second ch from hook, skip next st, sc in next st; rep from * across comb.

Fasten off.

Beak

Attach yellow yarn 8 sc away from comb.

Row 1: Ch 3, dc in next 3 sc. Turn.

Row 2: Ch 3, skip the first dc, dc2tog, dc 1 in top of ch-3 from prev row. Turn.

Row 3: Ch 3, skip first dc, dc2tog. Fasten off.

Eye

With black, ch 2, sc 10 in second ch form hook, sl st to join rnd. Fasten off.

Wing

Starting at pointed end, with color A, ch 4.

Row 1: Dc 2 in 4th ch from hook. Turn.

Row 2: Ch 3, dc 1, dc 3 in next dc, dc 2 in ch-3 from prev row. Turn.

Rows 3–6: Ch 3 , skip first dc, dc 1 in each dc across, [dc 3 in center of dc of dc-3 group from prev row], dc 1 in top of ch-3 from prev row. Turn.

Rows 7–9: Ch 3, skip first dc, dc 1 in each dc across, dc 1 in top of ch-3 from prev row. Turn.

Rows 10–11: Ch 3, skip first dc, dc3tog, dc in each dc to last 3 sts (counting ch-3 from prev row as a st), dc3tog. Turn.

Row 12: Ch 1, sc2tog, sc 1 in each st to last 2 sts, sc2tog.

Fasten off.

FINISHING

Block lightly, weave in ends. Sew eye to chicken, sew neck to body. Sew wing to body. ■

Tardy Turtle

TURTLE

Body (Worked in the Round)

Using MC and larger hook, ch 17.

Rnd 1: Dc 4 in 4th ch from hook, dc 1 in each of the next 12 ch sts, dc 5 in last ch, dc 12 along the back of the ch. Sl st into top of ch-3 to join rnd. Note that the ch-3 counts as a dc—34 sts.

Note: Work Rnds 2–8 in back loops of the prev rnd. Color A rings will be worked later in the front of the stitches.

Rnd 2: Ch 3 (counts as first dc), dc 1 into same st, dc 2 in next st, dc 1, [dc 2 in next st] 2 times, dc 12, [dc 2 in next st] 2 times, dc 1, [dc2 in next st] 2 times, dc 12, sl st into top of ch-3 to join rnd—42 sts.

Rnd 3: Ch 3 (counts as first dc), [dc 2 in next st, dc 1] 4 times, dc 12, [dc 1, dc 2 in next st] 4 times, dc 13, sl st into top of ch-3 to join rnd—50 sts.

Rnd 4: Ch 3 (counts as first dc), dc 1 into same st, dc 1, [dc 2 in next st] 2 times, dc 1, dc 2 in next st, dc 1, [dc 2 in next st, dc 1, dc 2 in next st] 2 times, dc 12, [dc 2 in next st, dc 1, dc 2 in next st] 2 times, dc 1, [dc 2 in next st, dc 1, dc 2 in next st] 2 times, dc 12, sl st into top of ch-3 to join rnd—66 sts.

Rnd 5: Ch 3 (counts as first dc), dc 1 into same st, [dc 1, dc 2 in next st] 4 times, dc 2, [dc 1, dc 2 in next st] 5 times, dc 12, [dc 2 in next st, dc 1] 5 times, dc 2, [dc 2 in next st, dc 1] 4 times, dc 2 in next st, dc 12, sl st into top of ch-3 to join rnd—86 sts.

Rnd 6: Ch 3 (counts as first dc), dc 1 into same st, [dc 1, dc 2 in next st] 5 times, dc 9, [dc 2, dc 1 in next st] 5 times, dc 2 in next st, dc 12, [dc 2 in next st, dc 1] 6 times, dc 8, [dc 2 in next st, dc 1] 5 times, dc 2 in next st, dc 12, sl st into top of ch-3 to join rnd—110 sts.

Rnd 7: Ch 3 (counts as first dc), dc around, sl st into ch-3 to join rnd—110 sts.

Rnd 8: Ch 3 (counts as first dc), dc 1 into same st, dc 2, [dc 2 in next dc, dc 2] 13 times, dc 12, [dc 2 in next st, dc 2] 14 times, dc 12, sl st into ch-3 to join.

Fasten off.

Head

Using MC and larger hook, ch 8.

FINISHED SIZE

9¼in/23.5cm high (from head to tail)
x 6in/15.25cm wide

YARN

DMC® *Petra Crochet Cotton Thread, Size 3*: 306yds/280m, 3.5oz/100g (100% mercerized cotton)—one ball: #5907 Green (MC)

DMC® *Cébélia Crochet Cotton Thread, Size 10*: 1.75oz/50g, 284yds/260m, (100% mercerized cotton)—one ball: #743 Gold (A)

Small amount of black embroidery floss

NOTIONS

• Size D/3 (3.25mm) and Size 6 (1.80mm) crochet hooks *or sizes needed to obtain gauge*

• Tapestry needle

GAUGE

24 sts and 28 rows = 4in/10cm over sc using MC and larger hook
Take time to check gauge.

Row 1: Sc 1 in second ch from hook, and in each ch st across. Turn—7 sts.

Rows 2, 4 & 5: Ch 1, sc 2 in first sc, sc across to last sc, sc 2 in last sc. Turn—9, 11, 13 sts.

Rows 3, 6, 7 & 9: Ch 1, sc across. Turn—9, 13, 11 sts.

Rows 8, 10, 11 & 12: Ch 1, sc2tog, sc across to last 2 sc, sc2tog. Turn—11, 9, 7, 5 sts.

Fasten off.

Legs (Make 4)

Using MC and larger hook, ch 8.

Row 1: Sc 1 in second ch from hook, and in each ch st across. Turn—7 sts.

Rows 2, 3, 5 & 7: Ch 1, sc across. Turn—7, 7, 5, 3 sts.

Rows 4 & 6: Ch 1, sc2tog, sc across to last 2 sc, sc2tog. Turn—5, 3 sts.

Attach color A to the front loop of the outer edge of Rnd 1. Using smaller hook, sc 1 in every st around, working at an even tension. Sl st into first sc to join. Fasten off. Repeat for every other rnd. Attach to last rnd, and sc 1 in front loop of every st around. Sl st to join. Fasten off.

Tail

Using MC and larger hook, ch 7.

Row 1: Sc 1 in second ch from hook, and in each ch st across. Turn—6 sts.

Rows 2, 3, 5, 6 & 8: Ch1, sc across. Turn—6, 6, 4, 4, 3 sts.

Row 4: Ch 1, sc2tog, sc across to last 2 sc, sc2tog. Turn—4 sts.

Row 7: Ch 1, sc 1, sc2tog, sc 1. Turn—3 sts.

Row 9: Ch 1, sc3tog.

Fasten off.

FINISHING

Rings on the Body

(Do not work these rounds tightly.)

Attach color A to a front loop of the outer edge of Rnd 1. Using smaller hook, sc 1 in every st around, sl st into first sc to join. Fasten off. Repeat for every other rnd. Attach to last rnd, and sc 1 in front loop of every st around. Sl st to join. Fasten off.

Sew head, legs, and tail to body.

Block lightly, weave in ends.

Thread tapestry needle with black floss, and embroider French knot eyes on either side of head. ▧

Beautiful *Butterfly*

BUTTERFLY

Body

Row 1: Using color A, ch 2, sc 3 in first ch from hook. Turn.

Row 2: Ch 1, sc 2 in first sc, sc to last st, sc 2 in last st. Turn—5 sts.

Row 3: Ch 1, sc across. Turn.

Rows 4–15: Repeat Rows 2 and 3—17 sts.

Rows 16–39: Ch 1, sc across. Turn.

Rows 40–42: Ch 1, sc2tog, sc across to last 2 sts, sc2tog. Turn—11 sts.

Rows 43 & 45: Ch 1, sc 2 in first sc, sc to last st, sc 2 in last st. Turn—13, 15 sts.

Rows 44, 46–50, 52, 53, 55, 56, 58 & 59: Ch 1, sc across. Turn.

Rows 51, 54 & 57: Ch 1, sc2tog, sc across to last 2 sts, sc2tog. Turn—13, 11, 9 sts.

Row 60: Ch 1, [sc2tog, sc 1] 3 times—6 sts.

Fasten off.

Wing (Make 2)

Commence at center edge.

Using MC, ch 20.

Row 1: Sc 1 in second ch from hook, sc across. Turn—19 sc.

Even Rows 2–26: Ch 1, sc 2 in first sc, sc to last st, sc 2 in last st. Turn—45 sts at end of Row 26.

Odd Rows 3–27: Ch 1, sc across. Turn.

Row 28: Ch1, sc 2 in first sc, sc 25. Turn—27 sts.

Rows 29, 31, 33, 35, 37 & 39: Ch 1, sc2tog, sc across. Turn—26 sts at end of Row 39.

Rows 30, 32, 34, 36 & 38: Ch 1, sc 2 in first sc, sc across. Turn—27 sts at end of Row 38.

Rows 40–44: Ch 1, sc2tog, sc to last 2 sts, sc2tog. Turn—16 sts.

Fasten off.

Skip one st in Row 28, and join MC in next st and sc 1 in each remaining sc to last st, sc 2 in last st. Turn—19 sts.

Rows 1, 3, 5, 7 & 9: Ch 1, sc to last 3 sts, sc2tog, sc 1. Turn—14 sts at end of Row 9.

Rows 2, 4, 6 & 8: Ch 1, sc 1, sc2tog, sc to last sc, sc 2 in last st. Turn—15 sts at end of Row 8.

Row 10: Ch 1, sc 1, sc2tog, sc to last 3 sts, sc2tog, sc 1—12 sts.

Fasten off.

Sew wings together at center edge.

Border

Attach MC to center seam at top, with RS facing, and sc around outside of butterfly as follows:

Rnd 1: Sc 40 along top of left wing, [sc 1, ch 1, sc 1] 3 times, sc 14; at corner, sc 1, ch 1, sc 1. Sc 15 along bottom side of top wing, sc3tog in inner corner, sc 9 along top of bottom wing; at corner sc 1, ch 1, sc 1. Sc 9; at corner [sc 1, ch 1, sc 1] 2 times, sc 36, sc3tog at inner corner, sc 36. At corner [sc 1, ch 1, sc 1] 2 times, sc 9, at corner sc 1, ch 1, sc 1, sc9 , sc3tog, sc 15; at corner sc 1, ch 1, sc 1, sc 14; at corner [sc 1, ch 1, sc 1] 3 times, sc 40, sl st to join. Fasten off.

FINISHED SIZE

6in/15cm high (from top to bottom of wing) x 9in/23cm (from left wing to right wing)

YARN

Coats & Clark *Aunt Lydia's® Classic™ Crochet Thread, Size 10*: 2.8oz/80g, 350yds/320m for solid colors A & B or 2.5oz/71g, 300yds/274m for multicolor MC (100% mercerized cotton)— one ball each: #154-995 Ocean (MC), #154-012 Black (A), #154-450 Aqua (B)

NOTIONS

• Size 6 (1.80mm) crochet hook *or size needed to obtain gauge*

• Tapestry needle

GAUGE

36 sts and 41 rows = 4in/10cm over sc
Take time to check gauge.

Rnd 2: Attach color A to last sc from prev rnd, sc2tog (the first and last sts of the prev rnd count as center top sc), sc 39, sk next sc, sc 3 in each of next 3 ch-1 sps, sk next sc, sc 14, sk next sc, sc 3 in next ch-1 sp, sk next sc, sc 14, sc2tog, sc 8, sk next sc, sc 3 in next ch-1 sp, sk next sc, sc 9, sk next sc, sc 3 in each of next 2 ch-1 sps, sk next sc, sc 35, sc3tog at center bottom of butterfly, sc 35, sk next sc, sc 2 in each of next 2 ch-1 sps, sk next sc, sc 9, sk next sc, sc 3 in next ch-1 sp, sk next sc, sc 8, sc2tog, sc 14, sk next sc, sc 3 in next ch-1 sp, sk next sc, sc 14, sc 3 in each of next 3 ch-1 sps, sk next sc, sc 38, sc3tog into last sc, the center top st and the first sc of next rnd.

Rnd 3: Sc 38, [sc 2 in next sc, sc 1, sc 2 in next sc] 3 times, sc 14, sc 2 in next sc, sc 1, sc 2 in next sc, sc 13, sc3tog, sc 7, sc 2 in next sc, sc 1, sc 2 in next sc, sc 9, [sc 2 in next sc, sc 1, sc 2 in next sc] 2 times, sc 34, sc3tog at center bottom of butterfly, sc 34, [sc 2 in next sc, sc 1, sc 2 in next sc] 2 times, sc 9, sc 2 in next sc, sc 1, sc 2 in next sc, sc 7, sc3tog, sc 13, sc 2 in next sc, sc 1, sc 2 in next sc, sc 14, [sc 2 in next sc, sc 1, sc 2 in next sc] 3 times, sc 38. Fasten off.

Antennas (Make 2)

Attach color A to last st at top of head and chain 10. Sc 1 in second ch from hook, sl st 8, sl st to head. Fasten off. Repeat on other side of head.

FINISHING

Block pieces lightly. Sew body to wings. ■

Organic *Orange*

ORANGE

Fruit

Using MC, make an adjustable loop.

Rnd 1 (RS): Ch 1, work 8 sc in the loop, tighten loop, join rnd with a sl st in first sc—8 sts. Turn.

Increase Rnd 2 (WS): Ch 1, work 2 sc in each sc 8 times, sl st into ch-1 to join rnd. Turn—16 sts.

Increase Rnd 3: Ch 1, [sc 2 in next sc, sc 1] 8 times, sl st into ch-1 to join rnd. Turn—24 sts.

Increase Rnd 4: Ch 1, [sc 2 in next sc, sc 2] 8 times, sl st into ch-1 to join rnd. Turn—32 sts.

Increase Rnd 5: Ch 1, [sc 2 in next sc, sc 3] 8 times, sl st into ch-1 to join rnd. Turn—40 sts.

Rnds 6, 8, 10, 11, 13, 14 & 16: Ch 1, sc 1 in each sc, sl st into ch-1 to join rnd. Turn—40, 48, 56, 56, 64, 72 sts.

Increase Rnd 7: Ch 1, [sc 2 in next sc, sc 4] 8 times, sl st into ch-1 to join rnd. Turn—48 sts.

Increase Rnd 9: Ch 1, [sc 2 in next sc, sc 5] 8 times, sl st into ch-1 to join rnd. Turn—56 sts.

Increase Rnd 12: Ch 1, [sc 2 in next sc, sc 6] 8 times, sl st into ch-1 to join rnd. Turn—64 sts.

Increase Rnd 15: Ch 1, [sc 2 in next sc, sc 7] 8 times, sl st into ch-1 to join rnd. Turn—72 sts.

Fasten off.

Orange Blossoms (Make 3)

Using color A, make an adjustable loop.

Rnd 1: Ch 1, work 10 sc in the loop, tighten loop, join rnd with a sl st in first sc—10 sts. Turn.

Rnd 2 (Petals): Ch 1, [sl st into next sc, ch 4 turn. Sc into second ch from hook, hdc 1 into next ch, dc 1 into next ch, sc 1 into next sc] 5 times, sl st into ch-1 to join rnd. Fasten off, leaving tail to sew to dishcloth.

Leaves (Make 3)

Using color B, ch 15.

Row 1: Sl st 1 in second ch from hook, sc 2, hdc 2, dc 4, hdc 2, sc 2, sl st 1, ch 1, commence work on other edge of foundation chain, sl st 1, sc 2, hdc 2, dc 4, hdc 2, sc 2, sl st 1, fasten off, leaving tail to sew to dishcloth.

FINISHED SIZE

7½in/19cm diameter

YARN

Premier® Yarns *Home Cotton*™: 2.8oz/80g, 140yds/128m (85% cotton, 15% polyester)—one skein each: #38-06 Orange (MC), #38-01 White (A), #44-13 Cucumber Lime (B)

Small amount of yellow yarn for embroidery

NOTIONS

- Size H/8 (5.00mm) crochet hook *or size needed to obtain gauge*
- Tapestry needle

GAUGE

15 sts and 17 rows = 4in/10cm over sc
Take time to check gauge.

FINISHING

Block lightly. Weave in ends. Sew leaves to top of orange, then sew flowers to orange. Thread tapestry needle with yellow yarn. Embroider French knots in the center of the orange blossoms. Make ring at top if desired as in the basic directions. ∎

Perky Pig

PIG

Body

Commence at backside.

Using MC, ch 12.

Row 1 (WS): Sc 1 in second ch from hook, and in each ch across. Turn—11 sts.

Increase Row 2: Ch 1, sc 2 in each of the next 2 sc, sc 7, sc 2 in each of the next 2 sc. Turn—15 sts.

Increase Row 3: Ch 1, sc 2 in each of the next 2 sc, sc 11, sc 2 in each of the next 2 sc. Turn—19 sts.

Increase Rows 4, 5, 9, 10 & 20: Ch 1, sc 2 in first sc, sc to last sc, sc 2 in last sc. Turn—21, 23, 25, 27, 35 sts.

Rows 6–8, 11–13, 16–19, 22–29 & 31–34: Ch 1, sc across. Turn—23, 23, 23, 27, 27, 27, 33, 33, 33, 33, 31, 31, 31, 31, 31, 31, 36, 36, 36, 36 sts.

Row 14 (leg): Ch 5, 2 sc in second ch from hook, sc 1 in each of next 3 ch sts, sc across. Turn—32 sts.

Increase Row 15: Ch 1, sc 2 in first sc, sc across. Turn—33 sts.

Increase Row 21: Ch 1, sc 2 in next sc, sc 29, ch 1. Turn—31 sts.

Row 30 (leg): Ch 5, sc 2 in second ch from hook, sc 1 in each of next 3 ch sts, sc across. Turn—36 sts.

Decrease Rows 35, 36, 38 & 42: Ch 1, sc to last 2 sts, sc2tog. Turn—35, 34, 27, 26 sts.

Row 37: Ch 1, sc 28. Turn—28 sts.

Increase Rows 39, 40 & 47: Ch 1, sc 2 in next sc, sc across. Turn—28, 29, 22 sts.

Row 41: Ch 1, sc 27. Turn—27 sts.

Decrease Row 43: Ch 1, sc2tog, sc across. Turn—25 sts.

Decrease Rows 44, 45, 50 & 51: Ch 1, sc2tog, sc to last 2 sts, sc2tog. Turn—23, 21, 15, 13 sts.

Rows 46 & 48: Ch 1, sc across. Turn—21, 22 sts.

Row 49: Ch 1, sc 17. Turn—17 sts.

Row 52: Ch 1, sc 8. Turn—8 sts.

Row 53: Ch 1, sl st 3, ch 1. Sc around entire pig for border.

Fasten off.

Tail

With MC, ch 15, sc 3 in second ch from hook, sc 3 in next 2 chs, sc 2 in each of remaining ch sts. Fasten off. Wrap the tail around a pencil to form it into a corkscrew.

FINISHED SIZE

7½in/19cm wide x 6in/15cm high

YARN

Coats & Clark *Aunt Lydia's*® *Fashion*™ *Crochet Thread, Size 3:* 1.76oz/50g, 150yds/137m (100% mercerized cotton)—one ball: #182-264 Lime (MC)

Small amount of black crochet thread

NOTIONS

- Size D/3 (3.25mm) crochet hook *or size needed to obtain gauge*
- Tapestry needle

GAUGE

23sts and 27 rows = 4in/10cm over sc
Take time to check gauge.

Ear

With MC, ch 11.

Row 1: Sc 1 in second ch from hook, and in each ch across. Turn—10 sts.

Rows 2 & 3: Ch 1, sc across. Turn—10 sts.

Decrease Rows 4–7: Ch 1, sc2tog, sc to last 2 sts, sc2tog. Turn—8, 6, 4, 2 sts.

Sc last 2 sts tog.

Fasten off.

FINISHING

Block lightly, weave in all ends. Sew ear and tail to pig.

Eye

Make an adjustable loop with black and sc 10 in loop, sl st to join rnd.

Next rnd: Ch 1, sc 2 in each sc from prev rnd. Fasten off.

Sew eye to pig. ■

Sweet *Strawberry*

STRAWBERRY

Fruit

Using MC and larger hook, ch 7.

Row 1: Sc 2 in second ch from hook, sc 3, [sc 2 in next ch] 2 times. Turn—9 sts.

Row 2: Ch 1, sc 2 in first sc, sc1 across. Turn—10 sc.

Rows 3, 10–12, 16–18, 20, 22 & 24: Ch1, sc 1 across. Turn—10, 21, 26, 24, 22, 20 sts.

Increase Rows 4, 9 & 14: Ch 1, sc 3 in first sc, sc to last st, sc 2 in last st. Turn—13, 21, 25 sts.

Increase Rows 5, 7, 8, 13 & 15: Ch 1, sc 2 in first sc, sc 1 across. Turn—15, 17, 18, 22, 26 sts.

Increase Row 6: Ch 1, sc 2 in first sc, sc to last st, sc 2 in last st. Turn—16 sts.

Decrease Rows 19, 21 & 23: Ch 1, sc2tog, sc to last 2 sts, sc2tog. Turn—24, 22, 20 sts.

Top Shaping (Each side is worked separately.)

Top Right

Row 1: Ch 1, sc2tog, sc 7, sl st 1. Turn—7 sts.

Row 2: Ch 1, sk the sl st, sc2tog, sc 4, sc2tog. Turn—6 sts.

Row 3: Ch 1, sc2tog, sc 3.

Fasten off.

Top Left

Attach MC yarn to base, one st away from the top right.

Row 1: Ch 1, sc 6, sc2tog. Turn—7 sts.

Row 2: Ch 1, sc2tog, sc 3, sc2tog. Turn—5 sts.

Row 3: Ch 1, sc 3, sc2tog.

Fasten off.

Leaves (Make 3)

Using smaller hook and Pearl Cotton #5, ch 26. Sc in second ch from hook, sc 1, dc 4, tr 12, dc 4, sc 3. Ch 1, and work next row along the back edge of the chain. Sc 4, dc 10, sc 11. Fasten off.

FINISHED SIZE
7¾in/19.75cm high x 6½in/16.5cm wide

YARN

Lily *Sugar and Cream*: 2.5oz/71g, 120yds/109m (100% cotton)—one skein: Red (MC)

DMC® *Pearl Cotton #5*: 27yds/25m (100% mercerized cotton)—one skein: #469 Avocado Green

Small amount of white yarn for embroidery

NOTIONS

- Size H/8 (5.00mm) and Size 4 (2.00mm) crochet hooks *or sizes needed to obtain gauge*
- Tapestry needle

GAUGE

13 sts and 14 rows = 4in/10cm over sc using MC and larger hook
Take time to check gauge.

Ring

Using smaller hook and Pearl Cotton #5, wrap yarn around 2 fingers 8 times for loop. Remove from fingers, and pinch to keep strands together. Sc over loop, packing stitches tightly together until loop is covered. Sl st into first sc to join. Fasten off, leaving yarn tail to sew to dishcloth.

FINISHING

Block lightly, weave in ends. Thread tapestry needle with white yarn and embroider straight stitch seeds. Sew hull/leaves and ring to strawberry. ■

LEAF

Center

Using MC, make an adjustable loop.

Rnd 1 (RS): Ch 1, work 8 sc in the loop, tighten loop, join rnd with a sl st in first sc—8 sc. Turn.

Increase Rnd 2 (WS): Ch 1, work 2 sc in each sc 8 times, sl st into ch-1 to join rnd. Turn—16 sts.

Increase Rnd 3: Ch1, [sc 2 in next sc, sc 1] 8 times, sl st into ch-1 to join rnd. Turn—24 sts.

Increase Rnd 4: Ch 1, [sc 2 in next sc, sc 2] 8 times, sl st into ch-1 to join rnd. Turn—32 sts.

Rnds 5 & 6: Ch 1, sc 1 in each sc, sl st into ch-1 to join rnd. Turn—32 sts.

Increase Rnd 7: Ch 1, [sc 2 in next sc, sc 3] 8 times, sl st into ch-1 to join rnd. Turn—40 sts.

Increase Rnd 8: Ch 1, [sc 2 in next sc, sc 4] 8 times, sl st into ch-1 to join rnd. Turn—48 sts.

Increase Rnd 9: Ch 1, [sc 2 in next sc, sc 5] 8 times, sl st into ch-1 to join rnd. Turn—56 sts.

Do not fasten off.

Top Peak

Row 1: Ch 1, sc 15.

Rows 2–5: Ch 1, sc 15. Turn—15 sts.

Row 6: Ch 3, dc 1 in first sc from prev row, [dc 1, hdc 1] in next st, hdc 1, sc 9, hdc 1, [hdc 1, dc 1] in next st, dc 2 in last st. Turn—19 sts.

Row 7: Ch 1, sl st 6, sc 7, sl st 6. Fasten off. Turn.

Attach yarn to first sc from Row 7.

Rows 8–10: Ch 1, sc 7. Turn—7 sts.

Row 11: Sl st 2, sc 3. Turn.

Row 12: Ch 1, sc 3. Turn—3 sts.

Row 13: Ch 1, sc3tog.

Fasten off.

Left Peak

With RS facing, reattach yarn into circle in sc to the left of top peak.

Row 1: Sc 12. Turn.

FINISHED SIZE

8in/20cm high (from center tip to bottom) x 7in/17.75cm wide (from tip to tip)

YARN

Knit Picks® Cotlin™: 1.75oz/50g, 123yds/112m (70% cotton, 30% linen)—one skein: #26994 Ivy (MC)

NOTIONS

- Size G/6 (4.00mm) crochet hook *or size needed to obtain gauge*
- Tapestry needle

GAUGE

17 sts and 22 rows = 4in/10cm over sc
Take time to check gauge.

Note:

Leaf is crocheted with a circle for the center, and 5 peaks are crocheted on the circle's outer edge.

Row 2: Ch 1, sc2tog, sc to last st, sc 2 in last st. Turn—12 sts.

Row 3: Ch 3, sl st in 3rd st from hook (picot made), sc 12. Turn.

Row 4: Ch 1, sc2tog, sc 9, sc 2 in next st. Turn—12 sts.

Row 5: Ch 1, sc 2 in first st, sc 9, sc2tog. Turn—12 sts.

Row 6: Ch 1, sc2tog, sc 9, do not work in last sc. Turn—10 sts.

Row 7: Ch 5, sl st in second ch from hook (picot made), dc 1 in first st from prev row, [dc 1, hdc 1] in next st, sc 1, sl st 3, sc 1, hdc 1, [hdc 1, dc 1] in next st, dc 1 in last st, ch 1.

Fasten off.

Right Peak

With WS facing, reattach yarn into circle in sc to the left of top peak.

Row 1: Sc 12. Turn.

Row 2: Ch 1, sc2tog, sc to last st, sc 2 in last st. Turn—12 sts.

Row 3: Ch 3, sl st in 3rd st from hook (picot made), sc 12. Turn.

Row 4: Ch 1, sc2tog, sc 9, sc 2 in next st. Turn—12 sts.

Row 5: Ch 1, sc 2 in first st, sc 9, sc2tog. Turn—12 sts.

Row 6: Ch 1, sc2tog, sc 9, do not work in last sc. Turn—10 sts.

Row 7: Ch 5, sl st in second ch from hook (picot made), dc 1 in first st from prev row, [dc 1, hdc 1] in next st, sc 1, sl st 1, sc 1, hdc 1, [hdc 1, dc 1] in next st, dc 1 in last st, ch 1.

Fasten off.

Bottom Left Peak

With RS facing, reattach yarn into circle in sc to the left of the left peak.

Row 1: Sc 7. Turn.

Rows 2, 4 & 6: Ch 1, sc2tog, sc 4, sc 2 in last st. Turn—7 sts.

Rows 3, 5 & 7: Ch 1, sc 2 in first st, sc 4, sc2tog. Turn—7 sts.

Fasten off.

Bottom Right Peak

With WS facing, reattach yarn into circle in sc to the left of the right peak.

Row 1: Sc 7. Turn.

Rows 2, 4 & 6: Ch1, sc2tog, sc 4, sc 2 in last st. Turn—7 sts.

Rows 3, 5 & 7: Ch 1, sc 2 in first st, sc 4, sc2tog. Turn—7 sts.

Fasten off.

Stem

With RS facing, attach yarn to st to left of bottom left piece. Sc 3. Work 4 more rows sc.

Next row: Ch 1, sc 2 in first sc, sc 1, sc 2 in next st. Turn—5 sts.

Sc 1 more row.

Fasten off.

FINISHING

Block lightly, weave in ends. ■

Handsome *Horse*

HORSE

Head

Using MC, ch 11.

Row 1: Sc 2 in second ch from hook, sc 8, sc 2 in last ch. Turn—12 sts.

Row 2 (RS): Working in the front loop, ch 1, sc 2 in first sc, sc across. Turn—13 sts.

Row 3 (WS): Working in the back loop, ch 1, sc 2 in first sc, sc across. Turn—14 sts.

Row 4: Ch 1, sc 2 in first sc, sc 11, sc2tog. Turn—14 sts.

Row 5: Ch 1, sc across to last sc, sc 2 in last sc. Turn—15 sts.

Increase Rows 6, 8, 10 & 12: Ch 1, sc 2 in first sc, sc across. Turn—16, 17, 18, 19 sts.

Rows 7, 9, 11, 13, 15–17, 20, & 23–25: Ch 1, sc across. Turn—16, 17, 18, 19, 19, 19, 19, 26, 24, 24, 24 sts.

Row 14: Ch 1, sc 2 in first sc, sc across to last 2 sts, sc2tog. Turn—19 sts.

Row 18: Ch 1, sc 18, sl st 1, ch 6, turn.

Increase Row 19: Sc 3 in second ch from hook, sc 1 in each of next 4 ch sts, sc 1 in sl st from prev row, sc across. Turn—26 sts.

Decrease Rows 21 & 27: Ch 1, sc across to last 2 sc, sc2tog. Turn—25, 22 sts.

Decrease Rows 22, 26, 28 & 30: Ch 1, sc2tog, sc across. Turn—24, 23, 21, 18 sts.

Decrease Rows 29 & 31: Ch 1, sc to last 4 sts, sc2tog 2 times. Turn—19, 16 sts.

Decrease Row 32: Ch 1, sk first st, sc2tog 2 times, sc to end.

Fasten off.

Ear

Note: Ear starts with a sl st.

Using MC, ch 12.

Set Up Row: Sl st in second ch from hook, sc 10. Turn—11 sts.

Row 1 (WS): Working in the back loop, ch 1, sk sl st, sc 2 in first sc, sc 7, sc2tog. Turn—10 sts.

FINISHED SIZE

7in/18cm high (from bottom of neck to top of ear) x 7½in/19cm wide (from back of neck to mouth)

YARN

Lion Brand® Yarn *24/7 Cotton*®, 3.5oz/100g, 186yds/170m (100% mercerized cotton)—one skein each: #761-124 Camel (MC), #761-110 Navy (A), #761-113 Red (B)

Small amounts of white yarn and black yarn

NOTIONS

- Size 7 (4.50mm) crochet hook *or size needed to obtain gauge*
- Tapestry needle

GAUGE

20 sts and 16 rows = 4in/10cm over pattern stitch (back and front sc variation)
Take time to check gauge.

STITCH GLOSSARY

Single Crochet Front and Back Variation

Odd numbered rows (RS): Work all sts in the back loop of the prev row.

Even numbered rows (WS): Work all sts in the front loop of the prev row.

Notes:

- The stitch variation gives a different st to row gauge than normal sc.
- For the horse's head, all even (RS) rows are worked in the front loop of the prev row, all odd (WS) rows are worked in the back loop of the prev row; for all stitches: single crochet, slip stitch, and sc2tog.
- The ribbed side is the back of the work.

Decrease Row 2 (RS): Working in the front loop, ch 1, sc2tog 2 times, sc 5, sc 2 in next st. Turn—9 sts.

Row 3: Ch 1, sc 2 in first sc, sc 7, sl st 1 in last st. Turn—10 sts.

Decrease Row 4: Ch 1, sk sl st, sc2tog 2 times, sc 5.

Fasten off.

Bridle

Front Piece (by mouth)

Using color A, ch 4.

Work 14 rows of 3 sc each. Fasten off. Thread tapestry needle with a 14in/36cm piece of white yarn; anchor yarn to bridle piece on back and weave the yarn under and over the middle stitch of the sc 3 rows to create a stitched effect. Fasten off.

Back Piece (by ears)

Using color A, ch 4.

Row 1: Sc 1 in second ch from hook, sc 2. Turn—3 sts.

Rows 2–7 & 11–17: Ch 1, sc 3. Turn.

Rows 8 & 10: Ch 1, sc 2 in first sc, sc2tog. Turn.

Row 9: Ch 1, sc2tog, sc 2 in last sc. Turn.

Fasten off. Thread tapestry needle with a 14in/36cm piece of white yarn, anchor yarn to bridle piece on back, and weave the yarn under and over the middle stitch of the sc 3 rows to create a stitched effect. Fasten off.

Long Cross Piece

Note: Make this piece as long as desired to fit across as shown in picture. (Thirty rows were used for the photo sample.)

Using color B, ch 4.

Row 1: Sc 1 in second ch from hook, sc 2. Turn—3 sts.

Rows 2–30: Ch 1, sc 3. Turn.

Fasten off

Rein

Using color B, ch 31.

Row 1: Sl st 1 in second ch from hook, sl st across. Fasten off.

FINISHING

Block lightly, weave in ends. Sew ear to head as in photo.

Mane: Using MC, cut 18–20 5in/13cm pieces of yarn. Fold each piece in half and secure to top of head using a fringe knot. Start mane 2 sts in front of ear and continue down top of head. Trim fringe. Fringe may be secured with stitching behind ear if desired.

Bridle and Rein: Stitch pieces of bridle to face as shown, and then stitch rein from bridle to back of neck.

Eye: Using black yarn, make an adjustable loop, and sc 8 into loop. Draw up to tighten, fasten off, leaving tail to sew down. Sew to head. ■

Amazing Acorn

ACORN

Bottom

Commence at bottom of acorn. Using MC, ch 36.

Row 1: Dc 1 in 4th ch from hook, and in each ch across. Turn—34 sts.

Note: Ch-3 counts as first dc.

Rows 2 & 3: Ch 3, dc 3 in first dc, dc across to last st, dc 4 in last st. Turn—40, 46 sts.

Rows 4 & 5: Ch 3, dc 2 in first dc, dc across to last st, dc 3 in last st. Turn—50, 54 sts.

Rows 6–19: Ch 3, dc 54. Turn—54 sts.

Switch to color A, attach thread to last dc.

Commence Cap

Row 1: Using color A, ch 5, dc 1 in 4th ch from hook, dc 1 in next st of ch (2 sts increased), dc in each of next 2 dc from prev row, popcorn st (PC) in next st, [dc 2, PC] 16 times, dc 1; in last st work, tr 1, [tr 1 into lower loop of prev tr worked] 2 times (increase of 2 sts made). Turn—17 popcorn sts made.

Rows 2, 4, 6, 8 & 10: Ch 1, sc across. Turn.

Row 3: Ch 3, dc in next sc, PC in next sc, [dc 2, PC] 18 times, dc 1 in last st. Turn.

Row 5: Ch 1, sl st over first 4 sc, PC in next sc, *dc 2, PC; repeat from * 16 times. Turn.

Row 7: Ch 1, sl st over first 3 sc, PC in next sc, *dc 2, PC; repeat from * 14 times. Turn.

Row 9: Ch 1, sl st over first 3 sc, PC in next sc, *dc 2, PC; repeat from * 12 times. Turn.

Row 11: Ch 1, sl st over first 6 sc, PC in next sc, *dc 2, PC; repeat from * 8 times.

Fasten off.

FINISHED SIZE

6in/15cm high x 6¾in/17.25cm wide

YARN

Knit Picks *Curio Cotton*, 3.5oz/100g, 721yds/660m (100% mercerized cotton)—one ball each: #26269 Spearmint (MC), #26263 Mongoose (A)

NOTIONS

- Size 1.75mm crochet hook *or size needed to obtain gauge*
- Tapestry needle

GAUGE

36 sts and 40 rows = 4in/10cm over sc
Take time to check gauge.

STITCH GLOSSARY

Popcorn Stitch (PC): Dc 5 in next st, drop loop from hook, insert hook from front to back in first of the 5 dc made, draw dropped loop through loop on hook—popcorn st made.

FINISHING

Point at Bottom of Acorn

With RS of work facing, attach MC to bottom of acorn, in first dc of first row, ch 1, and working along lower edge, sc 9, hdc 3, dc 2, tr 2, dtr 2, tr 2, dc 2, hdc 3, sc 9. Fasten off.

Block acorn lightly, weave in ends.

Top Loop

Using color A, make a hanging loop as in basic directions; sew to the center top of the dishcloth. ■

Orderly *Owl*

OWL

Body

Using MC, ch 20.

Row 1: Sc 1 in 4th ch from hook, [ch 1, sk next ch, sc 1 in next ch-1 sp] 8 times. Turn.

Row 2: Ch 3, [sc 1 in next ch-1 sp, ch 1] 8 times, sc 1 in ch-3 sp at end of prev row. Turn.

Increase Rows 3, 4, 6, 7, 9, 10, 13, 14, 30 & 31: Ch 3, * sc 1 in next ch-1 sp, ch 1; rep from * to ch-3 sp from prev row, [sc 1, ch 1, hdc 1] in ch-3 sp. Turn.

Rows 5, 8, 11, 12, 15–21, 24–29 & 32–34: Ch 3, *sc 1 in next ch-1 sp, ch 1; rep from * to ch-3 sp from prev row, sc 1 in ch-3 sp at end of prev row. Turn.

Decrease Rows 22 & 23: Ch, draw up a loop in each of the next 2 ch-1 sps from the prev row, yoh, and draw through all 3 loops on the hook (decrease made), *ch 1, sc 1 in next ch-1 sp; rep from * to ch-3 sp from prev row, sc 1, in ch-3 sp. Turn.

Row 35 (Make Ears): Ch 1, [dc 2, tr 4] in next ch-1 sp, [dc 1, hdc 2] in next sp, [sc next ch-1 sp, sc 1 in next sc] 2 times, hdc in next ch-1 sp, hdc 1 in next sc, [dc 1 in next ch-1 sp, dc 1 in next sc] 4 times, dc 1 in next ch-1 sp, hdc 1 in next sc, hdc in next ch-1 sp, [sc 1 in next sc, sc 1 in next ch-1 sp] 2 times, [hdc 2, dc 1] in next sp, [tr 4, dc 2] in next ch-1 sp, sc 1 in end ch-3 sp. Work sc around body to base of first ear. Join and fasten off.

Eyes (Make 2)

Rnd 1: Using black yarn, make an adjustable loop, sc 8 into loop, sl st to join rnd. Draw up loop to tighten. Switch to white yarn.

Rnd 2: Ch 1, working in back loop of prev rnd, sc 2 in each sc around, sl st into ch-1 to join rnd—16 sts.

Rnd 3: Ch 1, [sc 1, sc 2 in next sc] 8 times—24 sts.

Switch to Turquoise.

Rnd 4: Ch 1, sc 24, sl st to close rnd.

Fasten off.

Beak

Row 1: Using Carrot, ch 2, sc 1, in second ch from hook, turn.

FINISHED SIZE

8¾in/22cm high (from top of head to bottom) x 7½in/19cm wide

YARN

Premier® Yarns *Home Cotton*™: 2.8oz/80g, 140yds/128m (85% cotton, 15% polyester)— one skein #38-13 Pastel Blue (MC); small amounts of #38-12 Turquoise, #38-16 Black, #38-27 Carrot, #38-01 White

NOTIONS

- Size H/8 (5.00mm) crochet hook *or size needed to obtain gauge*
- Tapestry needle

GAUGE

15 sts and 17 rows = 4in/10cm over sc
Take time to check gauge.

STITCH GLOSSARY

Linen (Woven) Stitch: Using MC, ch an even number of sts—at least 8.

Row 1: Sc 1 in 4th ch from hook, *ch1, sk next ch-1, sc 1 in next ch; rep from * to end. Turn.

Row 2: Ch 3, *sc 1 in next ch-1 sp, ch 1; rep from * to end, sc 1 in ch-3 sp at end of prev row. Turn.

Row 2: Ch 1, sc 2 in sc from prev row.

Row 3: Ch 1, sc 2 in each sc from prev row. Turn—4 sts.

Row 4: Ch 1, sc 1, sc 2 in next sc, sc 2, sc 2 in next sc, sc 1. Turn—6 sts.

Work 2 more rows sc on 6 sts.

Fasten off.

FINISHING

Block lightly, sew eyes and beak to owl. Weave in ends. ■

Dandy Daffodil

DAFFODIL

Petals (Make 5)

Using MC, ch 13.

Row 1: Sk first ch, sc 1 in next ch, hdc 1, [dc 2 in next ch, dc 1] 4 times, hdc 1, sc 3 in last ch st, working along other edge of ch, hdc 1, [dc 1, dc 2 in next ch] 4 times, hdc 1, sc 1. Turn.

Row 2: Ch 1, skip sc, sc in next 3 sts, hdc 2, dc 9, dc 2 in next st, [dc 2, ch 3, sl st in last dc made (picot made), dc 2] in next st, dc 2 in next st, dc 9, hdc 2, sc 3, skip next sc, sc in center of end.

Fasten off, leaving tail to sew petals together.

Cup

Using color A, ch 2, sc 3 in second ch from hook. Turn.

Rows 1–3, 6: Ch 1, sc to last, sc 2 in last sc. Turn—4, 5, 6, 7 sts.

Rows 4, 5 & 7–9: Ch 1, sc across. Turn—6, 6, 7, 7, 7 sts.

Row 10: Ch 3 (counts as first dc), dc 1 in same st, hdc 1, sc 3, hdc 1, dc 2 in last st, drop color A, switch to MC. Turn—9 sts.

Create Frill

Using MC, ch1, and working in back loops, sc 1, hdc 1, dc 5, hdc 1, sc 1. Fasten off MC, and switch to color A. Sc around base of cup, up to other end of prev row. Sc 2 in first MC sc, [sc 1, sc 2 in next st] 4 times, then, in front loops of Row 10 sts, 2 sc in first st, [sc 1, sc 2 in next sc] 4 times. Sl st to first sc to join.

Next Rnd: [Ch 1, dc 1, ch 1, sc 1] 14 times. Fasten off.

FINISHING

Arrange petals by overlapping slightly. Tack in place and stitch together. Sew cup to petals. Block lightly, weave in ends. Make ring using green yarn, as in basic directions (see page iv). Sew to petal. ■

FINISHED SIZE

6in/15cm high x 8½in/21cm wide

YARN

Lion Brand® Yarn *24/7 Cotton®*, 3.5oz/100g, 186yds/170m (100% mercerized cotton)—one skein each: #761-157 Lemon (MC), #761-124 Camel (A)

Small amount of green yarn for loop

NOTIONS

- Size G/6 (4.00mm) crochet hook *or size needed to obtain gauge*
- Tapestry needle

GAUGE

17 sts and 21 rows = 4in/10cm over sc
Take time to check gauge.

Appealing *Apple*

APPLE

Fruit

Commence in the center with color A. Ch 6, join with sl st to form ring.

Rnd 1 (RS): Ch 3, dc 15 in ring, ch 3, sl st into ring.

Increase Rnd 2: Sc 5 into first ch-3 sp from prev rnd, sc 1 in each of next 5 dc, [sc 2 in next st] 2 times, sc 3 in next st, [sc 2 in next st] 2 times, sc 5, sc 5 in ch-3 sp, sl st into first sc to join rnd—31 sts.

Increase Rnd 3: Ch 1, sc 3, dc 11, dc 3 in next st, dc 11, sc 4, sl st in ch-1 to join rnd—33 sts.

Increase Rnd 4: Ch 1, sc 2 in each of next 3 sts, sc 11, [sc 2 in next st] 3 times, sc 11, sc 2 in each of next 3 sts, sl st in first ch-1 to join rnd—42 sts.

Rnd 5: Ch 3 (counts as first dc), dc 1 in second st and in each st around, sl st into top of ch-3 to join rnd—42 sts.

Switch to MC.

Increase Rnd 6: Using MC, ch 3 (counts as first dc) sk next st, dc 2 in next st, [dc 1, dc 2 in next st] 20 times, sl st into top of ch-3 to join rnd—63 sts.

Increase Rnd 7: Ch 3 (counts as first dc) sk next st, dc 1, dc 2 in next st, [dc 2, dc 2 in next st] 20 times, sl st into top of ch-3 to join rnd—84 sts.

Rnds 8 & 11: Ch 3 (counts as first dc) sk next st, dc 1 in each st from prev rnd, sl st into top of ch-3 to join rnd—84, 126 sts.

Increase Rnd 9: Ch 3 (counts as first dc) sk next st, dc 2, dc 2 in next st, [dc 3, dc 2 in next st] 20 times, sl st into top of ch-3 to join rnd—105 sts.

Increase Rnd 10: Ch 3 (counts as first dc) sk next st, dc 3, dc 2 in next st, [dc 4, dc 2 in next st] 20 times, sl st into top of ch-3 to join rnd—126 sts.

Increase Rnd 12: Ch 1, sc 3, hdc 2, [dc 2 in next st] 3 times, [tr 2 in next st] 5 times, [dc 2 in next st] 2 times, dc 32, dc 2 in next st, dc 3 in next st, dc 2 in next st, dc 26, dc 2 in next st, dc 3 in next st, dc 2 in next st, dc 32, [dc 2 in next st] 2 times, [tr 2 in next st] 5 times, [dc 2 in next st] 3 times, hdc 2, sc 3, sl st into ch-1 to join rnd—152 sts.

Switch to color B.

Rnd 13: Using color B, ch 3, sk next st, dc in each st around, sl st into top of ch-3 to join rnd.

FINISHED SIZE

5¾in/15cm high x 5½in/14cm wide

YARN

Coats & Clark *Aunt Lydias® Classic™ Crochet Thread, Size 10*: 2.8oz/80g, 350yds/320m (100% mercerized cotton)—one ball each: #154-1 White (MC), #154-423 Maize (A), #154-494 Victory Red (B), #154-449 Forest Green (C), small amount of #154-341 Russet (D)

NOTIONS

- Size 6 (1.80mm) crochet hook *or size needed to obtain gauge*
- Tapestry needle

GAUGE

36 sts and 41 rows = 4in/10cm over sc using 1.75mm hook
Take time to check gauge.

Fasten off.

Stem

Using color D, ch 27. Sc 1 in second ch from hook, sc 25. Ch 1, sl st 10, catch end of stem and sl st to form ring. Fasten off.

Leaf

Using color C, ch 20. Sl st 1, sc 1, hdc 1, dc 2 in next st, [tr 2 in next st] 2 times, tr 1, [tr 2 in next st] 2 times, dc 2 in next st, dc 4, hdc, sc 2, [sl st, ch 1, sl st] into last ch st, working along other edge of foundation ch, sc 2, hdc, dc 4, dc 2 in next st, [tr 2 in next st] 2 times, tr 1, [tr 2 in next st] 2 times, dc 2 in next st, hdc 1, sc 1, sl st 1. Fasten off.

FINISHING

Block lightly, weave in ends. Sew leaf and stem to apple. Thread tapestry needle with a 24in/61cm piece of color D thread, and embroider 2 lazy daisy st seeds. Stitch a straight st in the middle of each lazy daisy st. ∎

Snuggly *Scottie*

SCOTTIE IN PUFF STITCH

First (Right) Leg (Make 1)

Using MC, Ch 8.

Row 1 (RS): Sc 1 in second ch from hook, and every ch. Turn—7 sts.

Rows 2 & 4 (WS): Ch 1, sc 1, [ps 1, sc 1] 3 times. Turn.

Rows 3 & 7: Ch 1, sc 1 in each st across. Turn—7, 9 sts.

Increase Row 5: Ch 1, sc 6, sc 2 in last sc. Turn—8 sts.

Increase Row 6: Ch1, [sc 1, dc 1] in first st, [sc 1, ps 1] 3 times, sc 1. Turn.

Row 8: Ch 1, sc 1, [ps 1, sc 1] 4 times. Turn. Fasten off.

Second (Left) Leg (Make 1)

Ch 8.

Row 1 (RS): Sc 1 in second ch from hook, and every ch. Turn—7 sts.

Rows 2 and 4 (WS): Ch 1, sc 1, [ps 1, sc 1] 3 times. Turn.

Rows 3 and 7: Ch 1, sc 1 in each st across. Turn—7, 9 sts.

Increase Row 5: Ch 1, sc 2 in first sc, sc 6. Turn—8 sts.

Increase Row 6: Ch 1, [sc 1, ps 1] 3 times, sc 1, [dc 1, sc 1] in last st. Turn.

Row 8: Ch 1, sc 1, [ps 1, sc 1] 4 times.

Next Row: Ch 7.

Do **not** fasten off.

With WS facing, sl st 1 into the last sc of the first leg to join together the two legs and to form the bottom part of the body. Fasten off.

Body

With RS facing, attach thread to first sc of the right leg.

Row 1 (RS): Ch 1, sc 9, sc 1 in each of the next 7 ch sts, sc 9. Turn—25 sts.

Rows 2, 4, & 6 (WS): Ch 1, sc 1, [PS 1, sc 1] 12 times. Turn.

Rows 3 & 5: Ch 1, sc 1 in each st across. Turn.

Decrease Row 7: Ch 1, sc 23. Turn—23 sts.

Row 8: Ch 1, sc 1, [PS 1, sc 1] 11 times. Turn.

Decrease Row 9: Ch 1, sc 21. Turn—21 sts.

FINISHED SIZE

2½in/6.5cm tall x 7in/18cm wide (from tip of nose to end of body, not counting tail)

YARN

Coats & Clark *Aunt Lydia's® Fashion™ Crochet Thread, Size 3*: 1.76oz/50g, 150yds/137m (100% mercerized cotton)—one skein #182-201 White (MC)

Small amount of black yarn

NOTIONS

- Size D/3 (3.25mm) crochet hook *or size needed to obtain gauge*
- Tapestry needle

GAUGE

23 sts and 28 rows = 4in/10cm over sc
Take time to check gauge.

STITCH GLOSSARY

Puff Stitch (PS): Wrap yarn around hook, insert hook into next stitch, and draw yarn through. Wrap the yarn around the hook and draw through the first two loops on the hook. Two loops remain on the hook. Wrap yarn around hook, insert hook into the same stitch, and draw yarn through. Wrap the thread around the hook and draw through the first two loops on the hook. Three loops remain on the hook. Wrap the yarn around the hook and draw through the remaining three loops. Puff stitch made.

Notes:

- The firmer the tension of the adjoining sc st, the more the puff stitch will "puff."
- Each leg is crocheted separately. The designation first and second is used, as they will form the right and left leg respectively, once they are attached, and flipped over with the RS facing.

Row 10: Ch 1, sc 1, [PS 1, sc 1] 10 times. Turn.

Row 11: Ch 2, sc 1 into second ch from hook, sc to end. Turn—22 sts.

Row 12: Ch 1, [sc 1, PS 1] 10 times, sc 1, sc 2 in last sc. Turn.

Tail

Row 1 (RS): Ch 1, sc 9. Turn—9 sts.

Row 2 (WS): Ch 2, sk next 2 sc, [PS 1, sc 1] 3 times. Turn.

Row 3: Ch 2, sc 1 in second ch from hook, sc 6. Turn—7 sts.

Row 4: Ch 2, sk next 2 sc, [PS 1, sc 1] 2 times, PS 1. Turn.

Row 5: Ch 2 , sc 1 in second ch from hook, sc 5. Turn—6 sts.

Fasten off.

Head

Ch 12.

Row 1 (RS): Sc in second ch from hook and each ch across. Turn—11 sts.

Rows 2 & 4: (WS) Ch 1, sc 1, [PS 1, sc 1] 5 times. Turn.

Row 3: Ch 1, sc 1 in each st across. Turn.

Increase Rows 5, 7 & 9: Ch 1, sc to last st, sc 2 in last st. Turn—12, 14, 16 sts.

Row 6: Ch 1, [sc 1, dc 1] in next st, [PS 1, sc 1] 5 times, sc 1. Turn.

Attach black yarn to back of work.

Row 8: Using white yarn, ch 1, [sc 1, dc 1] in next st, [sc 1, PS 1], yoh, insert hook through next st, draw up yarn as if to make a single crochet—2 loops on hook. Drop white yarn to back of work, and using black yarn yoh, and draw through two loops on hook to complete the sc. Using black yarn, PS 1 (for eye), fasten off black yarn, resume with white yarn and complete row as established. Turn.

Row 10: Ch 1, [sc 1, dc 1] in next st [PS 1, sc 1] 7 times. Turn.

Row 11: Ch 1, sc 17. Fasten off.

Collar

Ch 26.

Row 1: Sc in second ch from hook and each ch across—25 sts. Fasten off.

FINISHING

Block lightly, weave in ends. Sew head to body.

Fold collar in half and place around neck. Sew seam to join. ∎

Proper *Penguin*

PENGUIN

Center Body

Using MC and larger hook, ch 30.

Rnd 1: Sc 3 in second ch (top sts), sc 27; sc 3 in last ch, sc 27 along back side of ch, sl st to join rnd.

Rnd 2 : Ch 1, [sc 1, sc 2 in next st] in each of the next 3 (top sts) sts, pm, sc 27, pm, [sc 1, sc 2 in next st] in each of next 3 sts, pm, sc 27, pm, sl st into ch-1 to join rnd.

Rnd 3: Ch 1, [sc 1, sc 2 in next st, sc 1] 3 times, sc 27, [sc 1, sc 2 in next st, sc 1] 3 times, sc 27, sl st into ch-1 to join rnd.

Rnd 4: Ch 1, [sc 2, sc 2 in next st, sc 1] 3 times, sc 27, [sc 2, sc 2 in next st, sc 1] 3 times, sc 27, sl st into ch-1 to join rnd.

Rnd 5: Ch 1, [sc 2, sc 2 in next st, sc 2] 3 times, sc 27, [sc 2, sc 2 in next st, sc 2] 3 times, sc 27, sl st into ch-1 to join rnd.

Rnd 6: Ch 1, [sc 3, sc 2 in next st, sc 2] 3 times, sc 27, [sc 3, sc 2 in next st, sc 2] 3 times, sc 27, sl st into ch-1 to join rnd.

Rnd 7: Ch 1, [sc 3, sc 2 in next st, sc 3] 3 times, sc 27, [sc 3, sc 2 in next st, sc 3] 3 times, sc 27, sl st into ch-1 to join rnd.

Rnd 8: Ch 1, [sc 3, sc 2 in next st, sc 4] 3 times, sc 27, [sc 3, sc 2 in next st, sc 4] 3 times, sc 27, sl st into ch-1 to join rnd.

Sides

Switch to color A. Mark center stitch at top and bottom of body. With RS facing, attach color A 4 sts away from center st.

Row 1: Using larger hook, and working in back loops of the prev rnd, sc 45. Turn.

Rows 2–7: Ch 1, sc2tog, sc to last 2 sts, sc2tog. Turn.

Fasten off.

With RS facing, attach color A yarn to corresponding spot on other side of body, and complete Rows 1–7. Fasten off.

FINISHED SIZE

9½in/24.25cm high x 4¼in/10.75cm wide

YARN

DMC® *Petra Crochet Cotton Thread, Size 3*: 3.5oz/100g, 140yds/280m (100% mercerized cotton)—one ball each: #B5200 White (MC), #5310 Black (A)

DMC® *Cebelia Crochet Cotton Thread Size 10*: 1.75oz/50g, 284yds/260m (100% mercerized cotton)—small amount of #743 Gold (B)

NOTIONS

- Size 6 (1.80mm) and Size D/3 (3.25mm) crochet hooks *or size needed to obtain gauge*
- Tapestry needle
- Locking clip stitch markers

GAUGE

24 sts and 28 rows = 4in/10cm over sc using MC and larger hook.
Take time to check gauge.

Note: Use stitch markers to keep count.

Head

Using color A, make an adjustable loop. Sc 7 in loop, draw up to close, sl st into first sc to join.

Rnd 1: Ch 1, sc 2 in each sc, sl st to join—14 sc.

Rnd 2: Ch 1, [sc 1, sc 2 in next sc] 7 times, sl st to join—21 sts.

Rnd 3: Ch 1, [sc 2, sc 2 in next sc] 7 times, sl st to join—28 sts.

Rnd 4: Ch 1, [sc 3, sc 2 in next sc] 7 times, sl st to join—35 sts.

Rnd 5: Ch 1, [sc 4, sc 2 in next sc] 7 times, sl st to join—42 sts.

Rnd 6: Ch 1, [sc 5, sc 2 in next sc] 7 times, sl st to join—48 sts.

Rnd 7: Ch 1, [sc 6, sc 2 in next sc] 7 times, sl st to join—54 sts.

Rnd 8: Ch 1, [sc 7, sc 2 in next sc] 7 times, sl st to join—63 sts.

Rnd 9: Ch 1, [sc 8, sc 2 in next sc] 7 times, sl st to join—70 sts.

Rnd 10: Ch 1, [sc 9, sc 2 in next sc] 7 times, sl st to join—77 sts.

Fasten off.

Eye

Using MC and larger hook, make an adjustable loop. Sc 6 in loop, draw up to close, sl st into first sc to join.

Rnd 1: Ch 1, sc 2 in each sc, sl st to join—12 sc.

Fasten off.

Using color A, and larger hook, make an adjustable loop. Sc 6 in loop, draw up to close, sl st into first sc to join.

Bow Tie

Using color A, ch 8. Sc 1 in second ch from hook, and each ch across—7 sts.

Sc 2 more rows. Fasten off.

Beak

Using color B and smaller hook, ch 11.

Row 1: Sc 1 in second ch from hook, and in each ch st across. Turn—10 sts.

Rows 2, 4, 6 & 8: Ch 1, sc across. Turn—10, 8, 6, 4, 3 sts.

Decrease Rows 3, 5 & 7: Ch 1, sc2tog, sc across to last 2 sc, sc 2 tog. Turn—8, 6, 4 sts.

Decrease Row 9: Ch 1, sc 1, sc2tog, sc 1. Turn—3 sts.

Decrease Row 10: Ch 1, sc3tog.

Fasten off.

FINISHING

Block lightly, weave in ends. Sew eye pieces together, and sew to head. Sew head to body. Attach color A thread to middle of bow tie piece, and wrap firmly around the center to create a bow. Sew to body. Thread tapestry needle with color A thread and embroider 3 French knot buttons down the middle of the body. Fold beak in half and sew along edge to join. Sew to head. ∎

BUSY Bumblebee

BUMBLEBEE

Stripe Sequence: [Sc 4 rows in color A, 4 rows in MC], sc 4 rows in color A.

Body

Commence Stripe Sequence at bottom of bumblebee. Carry color not in use along side of work.

Using color A, ch 13.

Row 1: Sc 1 in second ch from hook, and each ch across. Turn—12 sts.

Increase Rows 2, 4, 6, 8, 10, 12, 14 & 16: Ch1, sc 2 in first sc, sc across to last sc, sc 2 in last sc. Turn—14, 16, 18, 20, 22, 24, 26, 28 sts.

Rows 3, 5, 7, 9, 11, 13, 15 & 17–29: Ch 1, sc across. Turn—14, 16, 18, 20, 22, 24, 26, 28 sts.

Decrease Rows 30, 32, 34 & 36: Ch 1, sc2tog, sc across to last 2 sc, sc2tog. Turn—26, 24, 22, 20 sts.

Rows 31, 33, 35: Ch 1, sc across. Turn—26, 24, 20 sts.

Head

Switch to MC.

Rows 1: Ch 1, sc2tog, sc across to last 2 sc, sc2tog. Turn—18 sts.

Rows 2, 4, 6 & 8: Ch 1, sc across. Turn—18, 16, 14, 12, 10 sts.

Decrease Rows 3, 5, 7, 9, 10 & 11: Ch 1, sc2tog, sc across to last 2 sc, sc2tog. Turn—16, 14, 12, 10, 8, 6 sts.

Fasten off.

Wing (Make 1)

Using color B, ch 7. Sc 1 in second ch from hook, and each ch across. Turn—6 sts.

Increase Rows 1, 3, 5 & 7: Ch 1, sc 2 in first sc, sc across to last sc, sc 2 in last sc. Turn—8, 10, 12, 14 sts.

Rows 2, 4, 6, 8–11, 13, 15: Ch 1, sc across. Turn—8, 10, 12, 14, 14, 14, 14, 12, 10 sts.

Decrease Rows 12, 14 & 16: Ch 1, sc2tog, sc across to last 2 sc, sc2tog. Turn—12, 10, 8 sts.

Sc 1 sc all around. Fasten off.

FINISHED SIZE

7in/18cm high x 10in/25cm wide

YARN

Lion Brand® Yarn 24/7 *Cotton*®, 3.5oz/100g, 186yds/170m (100% mercerized cotton)—one skein each: #761-157 Lemon (MC), #761-153 Black (A), #761-100 White (B)

NOTIONS

- Size G/6 (4.00mm) crochet hook *or size needed to obtain gauge*
- Tapestry needle

GAUGE

17 sts and 19 rows = 4in/10cm over sc
Take time to check gauge.

Antennas (Make 2)

Ch 12. Sc 3 in second ch from hook, sl st to end. Fasten off, leaving tail to sew to head.

Eye (Make 1)

Make an adjustable loop. Into loop, sc 6, sl st into first sc to join. Fasten off, leaving tail to sew to head.

FINISHING

With RS facing, attach color A to bottom of head at left edge, and sc around entire body, ending at bottom of head at the right edge. Fasten off, and switch to MC. Sc from one side of head to the other. Ch 1, turn, sc 1 in each sc of head. Fasten off. Block lightly, and weave in yarn ends. Sew antennas, eye, and wing to bumblebee. ■

Cute *Cosmos*

COSMOS

Center

Using black yarn, make an adjustable loop. Sc 8 into adjustable loop, sl st to join, draw up loop to tighten.

Switch to color A.

Rnd 1 (WS): Using color A, ch 1, *sc 1 in back loop of next sc from prev rnd, in same sc st, dc2tog, rep from * 8 times, sl st into first sc to join rnd, turn—16 sts.

Rnd 2 (RS): Ch 1, working through both loops of the sts from the prev rnd, sc 2 in each st around, sl st into first sc to join rnd, turn—32 sts.

Switch to color B.

Rnd 3: Using color B, ch 1, *dc2tog in the back loops of the next sc, sc1 through both loops of the next sc, rep from * 16 times, sl st into first sc to join rnd, turn—32 sts.

Rnd 4: Ch 1, *working through loops of the prev rnd, sc 1 in next dc2tog, sc 2 in next st, rep from * around, sl st into 1 st sc to join rnd, turn—48 sts.

Rnd 5: Ch 1, *dc2tog in the back loops of the next sc, sc 1 through both loops of the next sc, rep from * 24 times, sl st into 1 st sc to join rnd, turn—48 sts.

Rnd 6: Ch 1, *working through both loops of the prev rnd, sc 2 in next st, sc 3, rep from * around, sl st into first sc to join rnd, turn—60 sts.

Fasten off.

Petals

With WS of center piece facing, attach MC to a sc st that is between any two dc2tog "puffs," ch 7, sk 1 ch, sc in next ch, hdc in next ch, dc 1 in each of next 3 chs, dc2tog in next ch, sk next st from center, sl st into next sc on the edge of the center piece. Turn. Ch 1, *working in back loops only, sk sl st, sc in next 4 dc. Turn. Ch 3, sk 1 ch, sc in next ch, hdc in next ch, dc in back loops of next 3 sc, dc2tog in next sc, sk one st on centerpiece, sl st into next st on edge of center piece. Rep from * around. End with sc row, and sew to first row to join.

FINISHING

Block lightly, weave in ends. ■

FINISHED SIZE

8in/20cm diameter

YARN

Premier® Yarns *Home Cotton*™: 2.8oz/80g, 140yds/128m (85% cotton, 15% polyester)—one skein each: #38-08 Pastel Pink (MC), #38-21 Lime Green (A), #38-09 Fuchsia (B)

Small amount of black yarn

NOTIONS

• Size H/8 (5.00mm) crochet hook *or size needed to obtain gauge*

• Tapestry needle

GAUGE

15 sts and 17 rows = 4in/10cm over sc
Take time to check gauge.

Note: Dc2tog are crocheted with the wrong side (WS) of work facing. They form "puffs" which show on right side (RS) of work. Work the sc sts between the "puffs" firmly to make the texture stand out more.

Delightful *Daisy*

DAISY

Center

Using MC, make an adjustable loop.

Rnd 1 (RS): Ch 1, work 7 sc in the loop, tighten loop, join rnd with a sl st in first sc—7 sts.

Increase Rnd 2: Ch 1, work 2 sc in each sc 7 times, sl st into ch-1 to join rnd—14 sts.

Increase Rnd 3: Ch 1, [sc 2 in next sc, sc 1] 7 times, sl st into ch-1 to join rnd—21 sts.

Increase Rnd 4: Ch 1, [sc 2 in next sc, sc 2] 7 times, sl st into ch-1 to join rnd—28 sts.

Increase Rnd 5: Ch 1, [sc 2 in next sc, sc 3] 7 times, sl st into ch-1 to join rnd—35 sts.

Increase Rnd 6: Ch 1, [sc 2 in next sc, sc 4] 7 times, sl st into ch-1 to join rnd—42 sts.

Increase Rnd 7: Ch 1, [sc 2 in next sc, sc 5] 7 times, sl st into ch-1 to join rnd—49 sts.

Increase Rnd 8: Ch 1, [sc 2 in next sc, sc 6] 7 times, sl st into ch-1 to join rnd—56 sts.

Increase Rnd 9: Ch 1, [sc 2 in next sc, sc 7] 7 times, sl st into ch-1 to join rnd—63 sts.

Increase Rnd 10: Ch 1, [sc 2 in next sc, sc 8] 7 times, sl st into ch-1 to join rnd—70 sts.

Increase Rnd 11: Ch 1, [sc 2 in next sc, sc 9] 7 times, sl st into ch-1 to join rnd—77 sts.

Increase Rnd 12: Ch 1, [sc 2 in next sc, sc 10] 7 times, sl st into ch-1 to join rnd—84 sts.

Increase Rnd 13: Ch 1, [sc 2 in next sc, sc 11] 7 times, sl st into ch-1 to join rnd—91 sts.

Increase Rnd 14: Ch 1, [sc 2 in next sc, sc 12] 7 times, sl st into ch-1 to join rnd—98 sts.

Increase Rnd 15: Ch 1, [sc 2 in next sc, sc 13] 7 times, sl st into ch-1 to join rnd—105 sts.

Increase Rnd 16: Ch 1, [sc 2 in next sc, sc 14] 7 times, sl st into ch-1 to join rnd—112 sts.

Increase Rnd 17: Ch 1, [sc 2 in next sc, sc 15] 7 times, sl st into ch-1 to join rnd—119 sts.

Increase Rnd 18: Ch 1, [sc 2 in next sc, sc 16] 7 times, sl st into ch-1 to join rnd—126 sts.

FINISHED SIZE

9in/23cm diameter

YARN

Coats & Clark *Aunt Lydia's® Fashion™ Crochet Thread, Size 3:* 1.76oz/50g, 150yds/137m (100% mercerized cotton)—one ball each: #182-423 Maize (MC), #182-201 White (A)

Small amount of black embroidery floss for embroidery

NOTIONS

- Size D/3 (3.25mm) crochet hook *or size needed to obtain gauge*
- Tapestry needle

GAUGE

23sts and 27 rows = 4in/10cm over sc
Take time to check gauge.

Rnd 19: Ch 1, sc 1 in each sc, sl st into first sc to join rnd.

Fasten off.

Petals (Make 14)

With RS facing, attach color A yarn to edge of daisy center.

Row 1 (RS): Sc 9. Turn—9 sts.

Rows 2–4, 6, 8: Ch 1, sc all sts. Turn—9, 9, 9, 7, 5 sts.

Row 5: Ch 1, sc 1, sc2tog, sc 3, sc2tog, sc 1. Turn—7 sts.

Row 7: Ch 1, sc 1, sc2tog, sc 1, sc2tog, sc 1. Turn—5 sts.

Row 9: Ch 1, sc 1, sc3tog , sc 1. Turn—3 sts.

Row 10: Ch 1, sc3tog. Fasten off.

FINISHING

Block lightly, weave in ends. Thread tapestry needle with embroidery floss, and embroider a back stitch mouth and straight stitch eyes. ■

CRAB

Note: When fastening off the various sections; leave a tail of at least 12in/30.5cm to sew the crab down to the base.

Dishcloth Base

Using MC and larger hook, ch 37. Work 42 rows in sc. Fasten off.

Border

Rnd 1: Attach MC to foundation chain row at bottom left corner. Sc 35 along foundation chain, [sc 1, ch 1, sc 1] in corner, sc 40 along next side, [sc 1, ch 1, sc 1] in corner, sc 34 along next side, [sc 1, ch 1, sc 1] in corner, sc 40 along next side, [sc 1, ch 1] in corner, sl st into first sc of rnd to join.

Rnd 2: Switch to color A, sc around working [sc 1, ch 1, sc 1] in each ch st of the prev rnd. Sl st to join.

Fasten off.

Crab Body

Using Color B and smaller hook, ch 2.

Row 1: Sc 2 in second ch from hook. Turn—2 sts.

Row 2: Ch 1, sc 2 in each sc. Turn—4 sts.

Increase Rows 3, 6, 7, 9, 10, 12, 13, 15 & 17: Ch 1, sc 2 in first sc, sc to last sc, sc 2 in last sc. Turn—6, 8, 10, 12, 14, 16, 18, 20, 22 sts.

Rows 4, 5, 8, 11, 14, 16, 18–26: Ch 1, sc 1 in each st across. Turn.

Decrease Rows 27, 29, 31, 32, 34, 35 & 38-40: Ch 1, sc2tog, sc across to last two sc, sc2tog. Turn—20, 18, 16, 14, 12 , 10, 8, 6, 4 sts.

Rows 28, 30, 33, 36, 37 & 41: Ch 1, sc 1 in each st across. Turn.

Row 42: Ch 1, sk 1 sc, sc, sc2tog, ch 3, dc in same space, sc all around, working 2 dc in opposite corner. Sl st to join.

Fasten off.

Front Claws (Make 2)

Using color B, ch 32.

Row 1: Sl st 1 in second ch from hook, sl st 1, sc 2, hdc 4, dc 10, sk next ch, hdc 2, dc 10. Turn.

Row 2: Ch 2, hdc 2, dc 2, tr 4, dc 3, hdc 1, sk next st, hdc 3, dc 6, ch 7, turn work, sl st 1 into second ch from hook, sl st 1, sc 2, hdc 2, sl st into base of next dc from prev row.

FINISHED SIZE

7in/18cm high x 7in/18cm wide

YARN

Coats & Clark *Aunt Lydia's® Fashion™ Crochet Thread, Size 3*: 1.76oz/50g, 150yds/137m, (100% mercerized cotton)—one ball each: #182-175 Warm Blue (MC), #182-201 White (A)

Coats & Clark *Aunt Lydia's® Classic™ Crochet Thread, Size 10*: 2.8oz/80g, 350yds/320m (100% mercerized cotton)—one ball: #154-494 Victory Red (B)

One skein six-strand embroidery floss in black

NOTIONS

• Size D/3 (3.25mm) and Size 6 (1.80mm) crochet hooks *or sizes needed to obtain gauge*

• Tapestry needle

GAUGE

23 sts and 27 rows = 4in/10cm over sc using size D/3 (3.25 mm) hook
Take time to check gauge.

Fasten off.

Legs (Make 6)

Using color B and smaller hook, ch 21. Sl st 1 into second ch from hook, sl st 1, sc 8, hdc 5, dc 5. Fasten off.

Front Legs (Make 2)

Using color B and smaller hook, ch 17. Sl st 1 into second ch from hook, sl st 2, sc 6, hdc 4, dc 3. Fasten off.

FINISHING

Block lightly. Baste or pin crab pieces to base, sew in place. Weave in ends. Thread tapestry needle with embroidery floss. Embroider French knot eyes and straight stitch antennas. ∎

Plucky *Pineapple*

PINEAPPLE

Commence at top.

Using color A, ch 13. Drop color A. Switch to MC.

Row 1 (MC): Working over color A, ch 3 (counts as first dc), dc 2 in 4th ch from hook (half shell made), sk 2 ch, sc in next ch, sk 2 ch, dc 5 in next ch (shell made), sk 2 ch, sc in next ch, sk 2 ch, dc 3 in last st (half shell made). Switch to color A. Turn.

Row 2 (Color A): Working over MC, ch 1, sc in first dc, sc in next 2 dc, sc in base of next sc (long sc made), sc in next 2 dc, sc 3 in next dc, sc in next 2 dc, long sc over next sc, sc in next 3 dc. Switch to MC. Turn.

Row 3: Ch 3, dc 2 in first sc, sc in next sc, shell in next long sc, sc in center sc of next shell, shell in next long sc, sk one sc, sc in next sc, half shell in next sc, switch to color A. Turn.

Row 4: Ch 1, sc 1 in first dc, sc in next 2 dc, *long sc over next sc, sc in next 2 dc, sc 3 in next dc, sc in next 2 dc; rep from * across, ending with a sc in the turning ch. Switch to MC. Turn.

Row 5: Ch 3 (counts as first dc), *dc 2 in first sc (half shell made), sc in next sc, shell in next long sc, sc in center sc of sc 3 group from prev row; rep from * across, ending with a shell in the last long sc, sk one sc, sc in next sc, half shell in last sc. Switch to color A. Turn.

Rows 6–11: Repeat Rows 4 and 5.

Row 12: Rep Row 4.

Rows 13, 17, 21 & 25: Ch 1, sc in first sc, half shell in next long sc, *sc in center of sc 3 from prev row, shell in next long sc; rep from * across, ending with half shell in last long sc, sc in last sc. Switch to color A. Turn.

Rows 14, 18 & 22: Ch 1, long sc over first sc, sc in next 3 dc, *long sc over next sc, sc in next 2 dc, sc 3 in next dc, sc 2; rep from * 5 times, long sc over next sc, sc 1 in each of next 3 dc, ending with long sc over last sc. Switch to MC. Turn.

Rows 15, 19 & 23: Ch 3, dc 2 in first long sc, skip 1 sc, sc 1 in next sc, *shell in next long sc, sc in center sc of next shell; rep from * 5 times, shell in next long sc, skip 1 sc, sc in next sc, half shell in last long sc.

FINISHED SIZE

6¾in/17cm high x 4½in/11cm wide

YARN

Coats & Clark *Aunt Lydia's® Classic™ Crochet Thread, Size 10:* 2.8oz/80g, 350yds/320m (100% mercerized cotton)—one ball each: #154-422 Golden Yellow (MC), #154-449 Forest Green (A)

NOTIONS

- Size 6 (1.80mm) crochet hook *or size needed to obtain gauge*
- Tapestry needle

GAUGE

36 sts and 41 rows = 4in/10cm over sc
Take time to check gauge.

Notes:

- Carry the color not in use loosely, and work the next row over the carried strand from the prev row.
- Switch colors by working last part of last st of each row in the new color.
- Half shell is comprised of 3 dc, or ch-3 (counts as first dc), dc 2.
- Long sc: sc in the base of the sc from the prev row.

Color Sequence: Work all odd rows in color A, even rows in MC.

Rows 16, 20 & 24: Ch 1, sc in next 3 dc, *long sc over next sc, sc in next 2 dc, sc 3 in next dc, sc 2; rep from * 6 times, long sc over next sc, sc 1 in each of next 3 dc. Switch to MC. Turn.

Rows 25, 27, 29, 31 & 33: Ch 1, sc 1 in first sc, half shell in next long sc, *sc in center of sc 3 from prev row, shell in next long sc; rep from * across, ending with, sc 1 in center of sc 3 from prev row, half shell in last long sc, sc 1 in last sc. Switch to color A. Turn.

Rows 26, 28, 30, 32 & 34: Ch 1, sc 1 in first dc, sc in next 2 dc, *long sc over next sc, sc in next 2 dc, sc 3 in next dc, sc in next 2 dc; rep from * across, sc 3 in last 3 sts. Switch to MC. Turn.

Fasten off.

Leaves (Make 5)

Using color A, ch 13.

Row 1: Sc 1 in second ch from hook, and in each sc across. Turn.

Row 2: Ch 1, sc2tog, sc across. Turn.

Row 3: Ch 1, sc across. Turn.

Rep Rows 2 & 3 until 1 st remains.

Fasten off.

FINISHING

Stack leaves together as shown, and sew to pineapple. Block lightly, weave in ends. ■

Radiant Rose

PINWHEEL

Using MC, ch 8, sl st to join ring.

Rnd 1: Ch 3, dc 17 in ring, sl st to join in top of ch-3—18 sts.

Work all following rnds in back loops only.

Rnds 2 & 3: Ch 3, dc 1 in ch-3 from prev rnd (counts as 2 dc), dc 2 in each dc around, sl st to join in top of ch-3—36, 72 sts.

Rnd 4: Ch 3, dc 5, ch 2, [dc 6, ch 2] 11 times, sl st to join in top of ch-3.

Rnd 5: Ch 3, dc 1 in ch-3 from prev rnd (counts as 2 dc), *dc 5, ch 2, dc 2 in first dc in next group; rep from * to end of rnd, ending last rep, sl st to join in top of ch-3.

Rnd 6: Ch 3, dc 2 in ch-3 from prev rnd, *dc 4, dc2tog, ch 2, dc 3 in first dc in next group; rep from * around, ending last rep, sl st to join in top of ch-3.

Rnd 7: Ch 3, dc in ch-3 from prev rnd, *[dc 2 in next dc] 2 times, dc 3, dc2tog, ch 2, dc 2 in first dc in next group; rep from * around, ending last rep, sl st to join in top of ch-3.

Rnd 8: Ch 3, dc in ch-3 from prev rnd, *[dc 2 in next dc] 2 times, dc 5, dc2tog, ch 2, dc 2 in first dc in next group; rep from * around, ending last rep, sl st to join in top of ch-3.

Rnd 9: Ch 3, dc in ch-3 from prev rnd, *[dc 2 in next dc] 2 times, dc 7, dc2tog, ch 2, dc 2 in first dc in next group; rep from * around, ending last rep, sl st to join in top of ch-3.

Rnd 10: Ch 3, dc 2 in ch-3 from prev rnd, *[dc 2 in next dc] 3 times, dc 6, [dc2tog] 2 times, ch 2, dc 2 in first dc in next group; rep from * around, ending last rep, sl st to join in top of ch-3.

Rnd 11: Ch 3, dc in ch-3 from prev rnd, *[dc 2 in next dc] 3 times, dc 8, [dc2tog] 2 times, ch 2, dc 2 in first dc in next group; rep from * around, ending last rep, sl st to join in top of ch-3.

Rnd 12: Ch 3, dc in ch-3 from prev rnd, *[dc 2 in next dc] 2 times, dc 11, [dc2tog] 2 times, ch 2, dc 2 in first dc in next group; rep from * around, ending last rep, sl st to join in top of ch-3.

FINISHED SIZE
8in/20cm high x 8in/20cm wide

YARN
Coats & Clark *Aunt Lydia's® Classic™ Crochet Thread, Size 10:* 2.8oz/80g, 350yds/320m (100% mercerized cotton)—one ball each: #154-661 Frosty Green (MC), #154-401 Orchid Pink (A), #154-1 White (B)

NOTIONS
• Size 8 (1.50mm) crochet hook *or size needed to obtain gauge*
• Tapestry needle

GAUGE
38 sts and 43 rows = 4in/10cm over sc
Take time to check gauge.

STITCH GLOSSARY

Dc2tog (Decrease): Wrap yarn around hook, insert hook into next stitch, and draw yarn through. Wrap the yarn around the hook and draw through the first two loops on the hook. Two loops remain on the hook. Wrap yarn around hook, insert hook into the next stitch, and draw yarn through. Wrap the thread around the hook and draw through the first two loops on the hook. Three loops remain on the hook. Wrap the yarn around the hook and draw through the remaining three loops. Decrease made.

Note: Circular increase pattern shifts during Rnd 11.

Rnd 13: Ch 1, sc in ch-3 from prev rnd, *hdc 2, dc 2 in next st, dc 1, [tr 2, tr 2 in next st] 2 times, tr 2, dc 2, 2 dc in next st, hdc 2, sc 1, sc 1 in ch-2 sp, sc 1 in first st of next group. Rep from * around, ending last rep, sl st to join in top of first sc.

Edge

Attach color B to sc between any 2 scallops. Ch 1, dc 4 in next sc, [sk 2 sts, dc 4 in next sc] 7 times. Now, working down left side of same group to center, [dc 4 in side of next row, around post of dc on edge of group] 9 times, sk next row, sl st around post of sc in next rnd (Rnd 2). Fasten off. Rep 11 times around circle.

Center Rose

Note: The rnds form a spiral and are not joined at the end of each rnd.

With color A, ch 8, join with sl st to join ring.

Rnd 1: Ch 1, sc 12 in ring. Sl st into first sc through back loop to join rnd.

Continue to work in back loops only.

Rnd 2: [Ch 1, dc 4 in next sc, ch 1, sc 1] 6 times.

Rnd 3: [Ch 3, sc behind petals in back loop of sc between next 2 petals] 6 times.

Rnd 4: [(Ch 1, dc 2, tr 2, dc 2) in next loop, ch 1, sc in sc between petals] 6 times.

Rnd 5: [Ch 5, sc behind petals in back loop of sc between next 2 petals] 6 times.

Rnd 6: [(Ch 1, dc 2, tr 5, dc 2) in next loop, ch1, sc in next sc] 6 times.

Fasten off.

FINISHING

Block lightly, weave in ends. Sew rose to center of pinwheel. ◼

Lovely *Ladybug*

LADYBUG

Commence at top of head.

Using color A, ch 6.

Row 1: Sc 2 in second ch from hook, sc 3, sc 2 in last ch. Turn—7sts.

Rows 2–8: Ch 1, sc 2 in first sc, sc across to last st, sc 2 in last st. Turn—9, 11, 13, 15, 17, 19, 21 sts.

Row 9: Ch 1, sc 21. Turn.

Switch to MC.

Rows 10–14: Using MC, ch 1, sc 2 in first sc, sc across to last st, sc 2 in last st. Turn—23, 25, 27, 29, 31 sts.

Rows 15–34: Ch 1, sc 31. Turn.

Rows 35–43: Ch 1, sc2tog, sc to last 2 sts, sc2tog. Turn—29, 27, 25, 23, 21, 19, 17, 15, 13 sts.

Switch to color B.

Rows 44 & 45: Using color B, ch 1, sc2tog, sc to last 2 sts, sc2tog. Turn—11, 9 sts.

Fasten off.

Dots (Make 6)

Using color B, make an adjustable loop, sc 7 into loop, sl st to join. Fasten off, draw up loop tightly. Leave tail to sew to ladybug.

FINISHING

Block lightly, weave in ends. Embroider or crochet a chain stitch line at center of ladybug's body using color B. Sew dots to body as shown in picture. ■

FINISHED SIZE
9in/23cm x 7in/17.75cm

YARN
Lion Brand® Yarn *24/7 Cotton®*, 3.5oz/100g, 186yds/170m, (100% mercerized cotton)—one skein each: #761-113 Red (MC), #761-153 Black (A)

NOTIONS
- Size 7 (4.50mm) crochet hook *or size needed to obtain gauge*
- Tapestry needle

Gauge
18 sts and 20 rows = 4in/10cm over sc
Take time to check gauge.

Gorgeous *Grapefruit*

GRAPEFRUIT

Using MC, make an adjustable loop.

Rnd 1 (RS): Ch 1, work 8 sc in the loop, tighten loop, join rnd with a sl st in first sc—8 sts.

Increase Rnd 2: Ch 1, work 2 sc in each sc 8 times, sl st into ch-1 to join rnd—16 sts.

Increase Rnd 3: Working in the back loops of prev round, ch 1, [sc 2 in next sc, sc 1] 8 times, sl st into ch-1 to join rnd—24 sts.

Increase Rnd 4: Ch 1, [sc 2 in next sc, sc 2] 8 times, sl st into ch-1 to join rnd—32 sts.

Increase Rnd 5: Ch 1, [sc 2 in next sc, sc 3] 8 times, sl st into ch-1 to join rnd—40 sts.

Rnds 6, 8, 10, 11 & 13: Ch 1, sc 1 in each sc, sl st into ch-1 to join rnd—40, 48, 56, 56 sts.

Increase Rnd 7: Ch 1, [sc 2 in next sc, sc 4] 8 times, sl st into ch-1 to join rnd—48 sts.

Increase Rnd 9: Ch 1, [sc 2 in next sc, sc 5] 8 times, sl st into ch-1 to join rnd—56 sts.

Increase Rnd 12: Ch 1, [sc 2 in next sc, sc 6] 8 times, sl st into ch-1 to join rnd—64 sts.

Rnd 14: With color A, ch 1, sc 1 in each sc, sl st into ch-1 to join rnd—64 sts.

Increase Rnd 15: With color B, ch 1, [sc 2 in next sc, sc 7] 8 times, sl st into ch-1 to join rnd—72 sts.

Fasten off.

Cherry

Using red yarn, make an adjustable loop.

Rnd 1 (RS): Ch 1, work 8 sc in the loop, tighten loop, join rnd with a sl st in first sc—8 sts.

Increase Rnd 2: Ch 1, work 2 sc in each sc 8 times, sl st into ch-1 to join rnd. Ch 8 (for stem).

Fasten off.

FINISHING

Block lightly, weave in ends. Thread tapestry needle with white yarn, and embroider 6 chain stitch lines for grapefruit segments. Stitch the cherry piece to the center section along the edge of Rnd 2 of the dishcloth. ■

FINISHED SIZE

7in/17.75cm diameter

YARN

Premier® Yarns *Home Cotton*™: 2.8oz/80g, 140yds/128m (85% cotton, 15% polyester)—one skein each: #38-04 Yellow (MC), #38-01 White (A), #44-13 Peach (B)

Small amount of red yarn for cherry

NOTIONS

• Size H/8 (5.00mm) crochet hook *or size needed to obtain gauge*

• Tapestry needle

GAUGE

15 sts and 17 rows = 4in/10cm over sc
Take time to check gauge.

PANSY

Note: All of the petals are worked separately into the same ring.

Using color B, ch 8, sl st to join ring.

Dark Petals (Make 3)

Petal base: Using color B, ch 3 (counts as first dc), dc 3 into ring. Fasten off.

Switch to MC.

Row 1: Ch 3, dc 2 in first st, [dc 3 in next st] 3 times. Turn—12 sts.

Rows 2 & 3: Ch 3 (counts as first dc), dc 2 in first st, dc across to last st, dc 3 in last st. Turn—16, 20 sts.

Rows 4–6: Ch 1, sc 2, hdc 2, dc 12, hdc 2, sc 2. Turn—20 sts.

Fasten off.

Attach MC to base of petal and sc along all three edges of petal.

Light Petals (Make 2)

Attach color A, ch 3 (counts as first dc), dc 3 into ring.

Row 1: Ch 3, dc 2 in first st, [dc 3 in next st] 3 times. Turn—12 sts.

Rows 2 & 3: Ch 3 (counts as first dc), dc 2 in first st, dc across to last st, dc 3 in last st. Turn—16, 20 sts.

Rows 4–6: Ch 1, sc 2, hdc 2, dc 12, hdc 2, sc 2. Turn—20 sts.

Fasten off.

Attach MC to base of petal and sc along all three edges of petal.

Fasten off.

FINISHING

Overlap petals to create a pleasing arrangement. Make sure that the center dark petal is on top of the surrounding petals. Stitch the petals to each other at the base. Thread a tapestry needle with color B yarn, and sew the center opening closed. Embroider straight stitches on the lighter petals. Using orange yarn, chain stitch around the edge of the color B center, and embroider straight stitches on the lighter petals. Block lightly, weave in ends. ■

FINISHED SIZE
8in/20cm high x 8in/20cm wide

YARN
Premier® Yarns *Home Cotton™*: 2.8oz/80g, 140yds/128m (85% cotton, 15% polyester)—one skein each: #38-17 Passionfruit (MC), #38-10 Lavender (A), #38-04 Yellow (B)

Small amount of orange yarn for embroidery

NOTIONS
- Size H/8 (5.00mm) crochet hook *or size needed to obtain gauge*
- Tapestry needle

GAUGE
15 sts and 17 rows = 4in/10cm over sc
Take time to check gauge.

Wild Watermelon

WATERMELON

Using MC, make an adjustable loop.

Rnd 1 (RS): Ch 1, work 8 sc in the loop, tighten loop, join rnd with a sl st in first sc—8 sc. Turn.

Increase Rnd 2: Ch 1, work 2 sc in each sc 8 times, sl st into ch-1 to join rnd. Turn—16 sts.

Increase Rnd 3: Ch 1, [sc 2 in next sc, sc 1] 8 times, sl st into ch-1 to join rnd. Turn—24 sts.

Increase Rnd 4: Ch 1, [sc 2 in next sc, sc 2] 8 times, sl st into ch-1 to join rnd. Turn—32 sts.

Increase Rnd 5: Ch 1, [sc 2 in next sc, sc 3] 8 times, sl st into ch-1 to join rnd. Turn—40 sts.

Rnds 6, 8, 10, 11, 13, 14: Ch 1, sc 1 in each sc, sl st into ch-1 to join rnd. Turn—40, 48, 56, 56, 64, 72 sts.

Increase Rnd 7: Ch 1, [sc 2 in next sc, sc 4] 8 times, sl st into ch-1 to join rnd. Turn—48 sts.

Increase Rnd 9: Ch 1, [sc 2 in next sc, sc 5] 8 times, sl st into ch-1 to join rnd. Turn—56 sts.

Increase Rnd 12: Ch 1, [sc 2 in next sc, sc 6] 8 times, sl st into ch-1 to join rnd. Turn—64 sts.

Increase Rnd 15: Ch 1, [sc 2 in next sc, sc 7] 8 times, sl st into ch-1 to join rnd. Turn—72 sts.

Fasten off.

Switch to color A.

Rnd 16: Ch 1, [sc 2 in next sc, sc 8] 8 times, sl st into ch-1 to join rnd. Turn—80 sts.

Fasten off.

Switch to color B.

Increase Rnd 17: Ch 1, [sc 2 in next sc, sc 9] 8 times, sl st into ch-1 to join rnd. Turn—88 sts.

Increase Rnd 18: Ch 1, [sc 2 in next sc, sc 10] 8 times, sl st into ch-1 to join rnd. Turn—96 sts.

Rnd 19: Ch 1, sc around, sl st to join.

Fasten off.

FINISHING

Block lightly, weave in ends. Thread tapestry needle with black floss. Embroider lazy daisy seeds, as shown in picture. ∎

FINISHED SIZE

7in/17.75cm diameter

YARN

Knit Picks® *CotLin*™: 1¾oz/50g, 123yds/112m (70% cotton, 30% linen)—one skein each: #24835 Cerise (MC), #24134 Swan (A), #24462 Sprout (B)

Small amounts of black floss for embroidery

NOTIONS

- Size G/6 (4.00mm) crochet hook *or size needed to obtain gauge*
- Tapestry needle

GAUGE

17 sts and 22 rows = 4in/10cm over sc
Take time to check gauge.

Leggy *Lobster*

LOBSTER

Note: When fastening off the various sections; leave a tail of at least 12in/30.5cm to sew the lobster down to the base.

Dishcloth Base

Using MC and larger hook, ch 37. Work 42 rows in sc. Fasten off.

Border

Rnd 1: Attach MC to foundation chain row at bottom left corner. Sc 35 along foundation chain, [sc 1, ch 1, sc 1] in corner, sc 40 along next side, [sc 1, ch 1, sc 1] in corner, sc 34 along next side, [sc 1, ch 1, sc 1] in corner, sc 40 along next side, [sc 1, ch 1] in corner, sl st into first sc of rnd to join.

Rnd 2: Switch to color A, sc around working [sc 1, ch 1, sc 1] in each ch st of the prev rnd. Sl st to join.

Fasten off.

Lobster Head/Body

Using color B and smaller hook, ch 16.

Row 1: Dc in 4th ch from hook and in each of next 11 ch sts, dc 5 in last ch, dc 12 along back side of ch. Turn—29 sts.

Row 2: Ch 3 (counts as first dc), skip first st from prev row, dc 12, [dc 2 in next st] 3 times, dc 13. Turn—32 sts.

Row 3: Ch 1, sc in first dc, [ch 8, sl st in 3rd ch from hook, ch 3, sl st in 3rd ch from hook, sl st in next 5 ch (creates leg), sc in the next 2 dc] 4 times, sc in the next 3 dc, ch 3, sl st in side of last sc just made (creates eye), sc in next 2 dc, ch 27, sl st in 2nd ch from hook, and in each sc across (creates feeler) sc 3, ch 27, sl st in 2nd ch from hook, and in each sc across (creates feeler) sc 2, ch 3, sl st into side of sc just made (creates eye) sc 5, [ch 8, sl st in 3rd ch from hook, ch 3, sl st in 3rd ch from hook, sl st in next 5 ch (creates leg), sc in the next 2 dc] 3 times, ch 8, sl st in 3rd ch from hook, ch 3, sl st in 3rd ch from hook, sc 1, sc in top of ch-3 from prev row.

Fasten off.

Medium Claw

Attach color B yarn to first sc following first set of legs made, ch 30.

FINISHED SIZE

7in/18cm high x 7in/18cm wide

YARNS

Coats & Clark *Aunt Lydia's® Fashion™ Crochet Thread, Size 3*: 1.76oz/50g, 150yds/137m, (100% mercerized cotton)—one ball each: #182-201 White (MC), #182-175 Warm Blue (A)

Coats and Clark *Aunt Lydia's® Classic™ 10 Crochet Thread* 350yds/320m (100% mercerized cotton)—one ball: #154-494 Victory Red (B)

1 skein six-strand embroidery floss in black

NOTIONS

- Size D/3 (3.25mm) and Size 6 (1.80mm) crochet hooks *or sizes needed to obtain gauge*
- Tapestry needle

GAUGE

23sts and 27 rows = 4in/10cm over sc using size D/3 (3.25mm) hook.
Take time to check gauge.

Row 1: Sl st in 2nd ch from hook, sc in the next 12 ch, (skip next ch, sc in the next 3 ch) 3 times; skip next ch, sc in each remaining ch, sl st into next 2 sc on body. Turn.

Row 2: Ch 1, sc in each sc across to last 11 sc, sl st in next sc, [(sl st in next sc, ch 3, and sl st into same sc), sl st into next 2 sc] 3 times, sl st in next sc, ch 3, and sl st (creates teeth).

Fasten off.

Row 3: With wrong side of last row facing, attach color B to 3rd sc following teeth, sc in next 3 sc, ch 15, sl st in 2nd ch from hook, sc in next ch, hdc in next ch, dc 2 in next ch, dc in next 2 ch, dc 2 in next ch, dc in next ch, hdc in each remaining ch. Sc 1 to join to claw, (sc3tog) 2 times, sc to end of claw, sl st to join to body.

Fasten off.

Large Claw

With wrong side of last row of body facing, attach color B to first sc following legs, ch 50.

Row 1: Sl st in second ch from hook, sl st in next 2 ch, sk next ch, (sc in next 5 ch, sc2tog) 4 times, sc in next 2-ch, sc2tog, sc in next 12 ch, sl st into next 2 sts on body. Turn.

Row 2: [Sc in next 3 sc, sc2tog] 2 times, hdc in next sc, dc in next sc, dc2tog, dc in next 3 sc, [dc2tog, dc in next sc] 6 times, sc2tog, sc in next 3 sc, sl st in next 3 sc. Turn.

Row 3: [Sl st in next st, ch3 and sl st, sl st in next st] 2 times, ch 3, sl st in 3rd ch from hook, sc in next 2 sts, [ch 3, sl st in 3rd ch from hook, hdc in next 2 sts] 2 times; dc in next 12 sts, ch 21, sl st in second ch from hook, sc in next ch, hdc in next 3 ch, dc in next 3, dc 2 in next ch, tr in next 5 ch, dc in next 6 ch, make a 5 dc cluster by making 2 dc in side of next dc, dc in base of same dc, and dc in next 2 sts, hdc in next st, sc in each remaining st, sl st into body.

Fasten off.

Tail

Starting at the lower end, using color B and smaller hook, ch 11.

Row 1: Dc in 4th ch from hook, dc in each ch across, 2 dc in last ch. Turn. Note that ch-3 at beginning of row counts as a dc st.

Row 2: Ch 1, sl st in back loop of each dc across. Turn.

Row 3: Ch 3, working in back loop of prev dc row, dc 2 in first st, dc in each dc across to last 3 dc, 3 dc in next dc. Turn.

Repeat last 2 rows 4 more times.

Fasten off.

Tail Fins

With wrong side of first dc row of tail facing, attach color B to first ch on opposite side of starting ch.

Row 1: Sl st in each ch across. Turn.

Row 2: Ch 4 (counts as first tr st), tr 4 in back loop of first sl st, tr in back loop of each sl st across, tr 5 in back loop of last sl st. Turn.

Row 3: Ch 1, sk first tr, sl st in next 2 tr, [sc 1, hdc 2, sc 1 in next tr], hdc in next tr, dc in next tr, tr 3 in next tr, dc in next tr, hdc in next tr, [sc 1, hdc 2, sc 1 in last tr].

Fasten off.

FINISHING

Block lightly. Baste or pin lobster pieces to base, sew in place. Weave in ends. Thread tapestry needle with embroidery floss. Embroider French knot eyes right over crocheted eyes. ■